THE FIRST RAINBOW

The First Rainbow

Favorite Bible Stories
to Learn From

by

John Calvin Reid

illustrated by

Edward J. Riojas

William B. Eerdmans Publishing Company
Grand Rapids, Michigan

A number of these stories have appeared in slightly different form in an earlier volume by John Calvin Reid entitled *Thirty Favorite Bible Stories*, published by Standard Publishing Company of Cincinnati, Ohio.

To Marty, Meara, and Jonathan
from their loving grandfather

Contents

Preface

In retelling these stories of the Bible, my first aim has been to make them *interesting*. To capture and hold the attention of children, I have given free rein to imagination, being careful all the while to observe a reverent regard for the inspired original record.

My second aim has been to make these stories *practical*. This is the reason for the introduction, the brief prayer, and the discussion questions that accompany each story. I hope that teachers and students in the classroom, as well as parents and children in the home, will discover and apply the important spiritual and moral truths which lie, partly revealed and partly concealed, between the lines of each story.

In short, these stories are intended to *teach* as well as to *entertain!*

J. C. R.

Introduction

In my boyhood days,
Which long ago sped,
A Bible with pictures
Was beside my bed.

Each night a chapter
I tried to read;
Thus in my heart
To plant a good seed.

Some pages seemed dull,
I must admit;
But others so lively,
'Twas hard to quit.

The stories I liked,
I've rewritten for you;
I hope you'll love them,
As I still do.

The Author

The First Rainbow

Genesis 6–9

What's the most beautiful sight you've ever seen in the sky? A rainbow? The next time you see a bright one, try to count the colors. There should be seven: red, orange, yellow, green, blue, indigo, and purple.

Do you know what makes a rainbow? Not rain by itself, but the sun shining through the rain after the cloud has passed on. So the rainbow is usually a sign that the storm is over. But the rainbow is also a very important sign of a promise made long ago.

❧   ❧   ❧

Suppose you were an artist and had finished a beautiful picture. Then suppose something bad happened to it — suppose someone broke in and splashed paint all over it! What would you do with your ruined picture? You would probably throw it away and start over, wouldn't you? According to the Bible, there was a time when God felt very much the same way about the world he had made.

At the beginning, everything was lovely, and God was pleased. The Bible says it like this: "God looked upon everything that He had made, and, behold, it was very good."

But later, people became very wicked. Not only were they wicked in what they did and said, but their thoughts were evil too. They hated one another. God felt very sad about this and decided to send a flood to destroy the world. Then he would start over.

But there was one man who wasn't wicked. Noah was his name. He obeyed God's commandments, taught them to his children, and lived close to God every day.

So God said to him, "Noah, there is too much hate and violence in the world. I'm going to send a flood to destroy it. But because you are a good man and have always obeyed my commandments, I'm going to save you and your family. Listen as I tell you what to do."

Then God told Noah to get busy and build a ship, which in those days was called an ark. God told him what kind of wood to use, what size to make it, and how to seal it with tar so it would float when the flood came.

So Noah and his sons began building the ark. Noah's neighbors made fun of him and called him names as they watched him and his sons working on the ark day after day, year after year, and talking about a flood coming when there wasn't a cloud in the sky. But that didn't bother Noah. He knew he was doing what God had told him to do.

Finally the ark was finished. God told Noah to put a supply of food in the ark, and also to take into the ark animals and birds of every kind, both males and females, so they wouldn't drown in the flood.

In all these things, Noah did exactly what God told him to do.

Then he and his wife and his three sons and their wives went into the ark, and God shut the door.

Before long, the clouds came and the rain began to fall. It kept pouring down in great torrents for forty days and forty nights, until the land was covered everywhere. Even the mountains were underwater. When at last the rain stopped and the skies cleared, there was no land to be seen anywhere. But the ark still floated safely on top of the water.

Eventually, after several months, the ark landed on a mountain called Ararat. Noah waited a few months to let the waters drain away from the earth. Then he sent out a dove to find out if the waters had dried up. The dove flew here and there, but could find no place to land, so she returned to the ark.

Noah waited another week, and then sent the dove out again. Late that evening she came back, this time with an olive leaf in her mouth. The leaf was freshly picked from a tree, so Noah and his family knew the waters were beginning to dry up and the land was beginning to appear. Again Noah waited a week and sent the dove out a third time. This time she didn't return. The land was dry!

Then God said to Noah, "Go out now, you and your family and also all the birds and animals that have been saved from the flood." So Noah opened the door of the ark, and he and his family came out. Then out came the "families" of animals and birds.

Can you guess the first thing that Noah and his family did? They built an altar and prepared to pray because they were so grateful! Then, kneeling around the altar, they thanked God for his great kindness in saving them from the flood.

When they finished praying, they looked up, and what do you suppose they saw in the sky? A glorious rainbow!

And God said to Noah, "The rainbow is a sign of the promise I now make to you and your children, that never again will there be a flood that will destroy the whole earth. While the world lasts, there will be planting time and harvest time, summer and winter, and day and night. The rainbow is my sign that I will keep my promise."

Since the time of Noah and his family, the rainbow has been a sign of this promise, what is called a covenant. The next time you see a beautiful rainbow in the sky, remember what it means.

Prayer

Dear God, how many beautiful things there are in the world around us and in the sky above us that speak to us of your greatness, your power, and your love!

Help us not only to notice these things, but to praise you for them and to be truly thankful for your great goodness to us. In Jesus' name, amen.

Questions

1. How did God feel about the wickedness he saw in the world in the time of Noah?
2. How was Noah different from the other people who lived at that time?
3. Do you think those people could have done something that might

have influenced God to "change his mind" and not send the flood? If so, what? (See Jonah, chapter 3.)

4. How do you think God feels about the wickedness he sees in the world today?

5. In what ways are we responsible for it, and what should we do?

6. What do you think God was doing about the wickedness in the world when he sent Jesus?

7. Of what promise of God does the rainbow remind us? Can you think of other promises of his?

8. What is your part in helping God's promises to come true?

9. Can you think of some promises you should make to God?

A Cheater's Dream

Genesis 27; 28:10-22; 32:27-28

Suppose you did something that was very wrong, and you knew you should be punished. But instead of punishing you, your parents forgave you and told you how very special you were to them. How would you feel? Would you be so relieved and thankful that you would try to be a better person ever after?

If so, you will understand how Jacob felt after his wonderful dream. But that isn't where the story begins.

❧ ❧ ❧

Jacob and Esau were twin brothers, but Esau had been born first. In those days, that meant that one day he would get more of their father's property than Jacob would. This was called his "birthright." As the boys grew up, it was clear that they were very different. Esau loved to be outdoors and became a good hunter. But Jacob liked to stay at home. He even learned to cook.

One afternoon Jacob had a pot of meat and vegetables boiling when Esau came in from hunting. Esau was very tired and hungry. When he saw Jacob's stew, his mouth began to water. He said, "That smells good. Give me some before I faint; I'm starving!"

Jacob saw his chance to get ahead of his brother: "You may have all you can eat, if you sell me your birthright first."

Esau thought, "What good will my birthright be to me if I die from hunger?" So he agreed to the deal Jacob offered. How foolish he was to sell his birthright for one meal! But how selfish Jacob was!

Of course, Esau and Jacob did not tell their father Isaac about this agreement. Years went by, and Isaac became old and blind; he didn't know how much longer he would live. One day he called for Esau and said, "My son, take your bow and arrows, go out into the field, and hunt game for me. Then bring it home and cook me a meal such as I like, and I will give you my blessing and your birthright."

But Jacob saw a way to trick his father before Esau came back from hunting. He killed two little goats from the flock, and, with his mother's help, he cooked the kind of meal that Isaac liked and carried it in to him, pretending that he was Esau. He even wore Esau's clothes and wore the skins of the goats on his hands and neck so he would seem hairy like his brother.

Isaac wondered how Esau could be back from hunting so soon. "Are you really my son, Esau?" he asked.

Jacob answered him with an out-and-out lie. "Yes, I am," he said. When Isaac asked Jacob to come close to him so that he could touch him and know who he was, he was fooled by the goatskins Jacob was wearing. He thought he was touching Esau's hairy hands.

Then Isaac gave Jacob the blessing that he thought he was giving to Esau. So, for a second time, Jacob had cheated his brother. After

Now we come to Jacob's first night away from home. He had no place to sleep except outdoors. So after the sun had set, he found himself a big smooth rock for a pillow and lay down under the stars. And as he slept, he had a dream.

What kind of dream do you suppose it was? A bad dream? A

nightmare? That is surely the kind of dream he deserved because of the way he had treated his brother! But how thankful all of us should be that God treats us better than we deserve. That was the way God treated Jacob on his first night away from home: he came to him in a truly wonderful dream!

In that dream, Jacob saw a long ladder set up on the earth. The top of it reached all the way to heaven, and angels were moving up and down on it. Above it, God was standing, and he said to Jacob, "I am the God of your grandfather Abraham and of your father Isaac, and I will be your God also. The land on which you are lying I will give to you and to your descendants, to your children and your grandchildren. And through you and your descendants, I will bless all the nations of the earth. I will be with you and keep you wherever you go, and I will bring you back to this land. I will never leave you until I have done all that I have promised."

That was truly a wonderful dream — just the opposite of what Jacob deserved. It's no wonder that when he woke up, he said, "Surely the Lord is in this place. This is none other than the house of God, and this is the gate of heaven." Then he named the place Bethel, which means "God's house." Before Jacob left to go on his way, he set up the stone he had put under his head as a monument and made a solemn promise to God: "Of all that you give me, I will give back one tenth to you."

Jacob was changed by the dream he had at Bethel. Then and there he began to become a different and better man. Some twenty years later, God came to him again and said, "Your name will not be Jacob anymore — it will be Israel."

Just how different he had become by that time you can judge for yourself when I tell you that his old name, Jacob, means "Cheater," while the new name God gave him, Israel, means "God's Prince."

Prayer

Dear God, many times you have treated me so much better than I deserve — just as you did Jacob. Make me truly thankful for how good you are to me, and help me to prove how thankful I am by being the kind of person you want me to be. In Jesus' name, amen.

Questions

1. Describe how Jacob cheated his brother Esau.
2. How do you feel when someone tricks you or cheats you?
3. Why did Jacob leave home?
4. Describe Jacob's dream and the promise God made to him.
5. What promises do you know of that God has made to you?
6. What promise did Jacob make to God?
7. How do we know that Jacob later became a different and better man?
8. Do you think God is trying to make you a better person too? How?
9. What can you do to allow God to make you a better person?

The Cheater's Fear

Genesis 32:1-21; 33:1-11

Which do you think is harder: to say "I'm sorry" and ask someone to forgive you; or to say "That's O.K." and forgive and forget? Well, neither is easy, is it?

But how unhappy two people can be when one has done a wrong against the other and neither tries to make it right. And what relief and joy both people feel when they finally get together and make up. The Bible tells us about two brothers who did just that.

❧   ❧   ❧

The servant was trembling as he rushed into Jacob's tent. "My lord, your brother Esau is coming!" he said. "Look, on yonder hill, you can see him, and with him are four hundred men!" Then Jacob was frightened too. He remembered as though it were yesterday how he had cheated his brother twenty years ago.

To escape from Esau's anger, Jacob had run away to the land of

Paddan-aram. There he had lived for twenty years with his uncle Laban. He had married and had become the father of twelve sons and one daughter. He also had become quite wealthy: he had large flocks of sheep and goats. Now, with all his possessions and his family, he was coming back, as God had commanded him, to the land where he had been born.

No wonder he was afraid when he saw Esau coming with four hundred men! The wrong he had done to his brother twenty years earlier had never been set right. It was his guilty conscience that made him afraid. And Esau had said he would kill Jacob!

But though he was afraid, Jacob did a very wise thing. He turned to God in prayer and said, "O God, I am not worthy of even the smallest of your blessings. Truly you have been good and kind to me. I had nothing but a staff in my hand when I left my home twenty years ago. Now, as I come back, I have a great flock of sheep and goats. You said to me, 'Come back to your country and to your people,' and you promised, 'I will deal well with you.' So save me and my family from Esau now, I pray, and let me receive grace and forgiveness from him."

When he had finished praying, Jacob hurried to send not one but five generous presents to Esau. He ordered his servants to take with them, group by group, with a space between each group, 220 goats, 220 sheep, 60 camels, 50 cows, and 30 donkeys. Jacob and his family followed after the last group of animals.

As each servant approached Esau, he bowed and repeated what Jacob had told him to say: "These are from your brother Jacob, a present to you, my lord. And he himself is coming to greet you."

When at last Jacob and his family came into view, Esau ran to meet him, not in anger but in forgiveness. Esau threw his arms around Jacob and kissed him. As they wept upon each other's shoulder, Esau asked, "Why have you sent me all these animals?"

"They are a present for you, my brother, because I wanted you to forgive me."

"But I have enough," Esau answered, "and no present is needed, dear brother. Keep your flocks and herds for yourself. I have already forgiven you."

But Jacob insisted: "Then accept my present as an expression of my gratitude, my brother. You have been so very kind and forgiving that looking into your face is like seeing the face of God."

Wasn't that a wonderful thing for Jacob to say? And also how true! So Esau and Jacob became true brothers again, in this way showing to the world what a beautiful thing it is to forgive and forget.

We too help others to see what God is like when we are forgiving and kind to those who have done wrong to us.

Prayer

Dear God, if anyone has done a wrong against me, help me to forgive and to forget and to treat that person as if nothing had ever come between us. And if I have done a wrong against someone else, give me the courage to say "I'm sorry" and to ask to be forgiven.

May I always be kind to the members of my family and my friends, tenderhearted and forgiving as you have always been to me. In Jesus' name, amen.

Questions

1. Why was Jacob afraid of Esau? What did he do to try to win Esau's goodwill?
2. Can you think of anyone you should "go to meet" as Esau "went to meet" Jacob? Will you do it?
3. Which is harder for you: to apologize and ask to be forgiven, or to accept an apology and forgive?
4. What do you think makes a good apology?
5. What do you think of someone who says, "I forgive, but I can't forget"?
6. If we are not willing to forgive someone, what do you think we are

asking for when we pray, "Forgive us our debts, as we forgive our debtors"?

* For another beautiful story of forgiveness in your Bible, read Luke 15:11-24.

Down with the Dreamer!

Genesis 37; 39:1-6

How do you feel about dreams? Do you think they tell something about the future? There was a time when people thought a good dream meant something good was going to happen, and a bad dream meant trouble was ahead.

Once there was a boy who dreamed that someday he would be great and famous. It was a long time before that dream came true, but it finally did! In the years before it came true, many things that were hard to take happened to that boy. But through them all, he kept his faith in God, and God made them work together for *good*.

God still has a way of bringing good out of bad for those who trust him.

❧　　　❧　　　❧

Joseph was next to the youngest son in a family of twelve brothers and one sister. His father, Jacob, loved Joseph more than the other brothers, and they knew it and didn't like Joseph at all.

Another reason Joseph's brothers hated him was because of his dreams. One day Joseph said to his brothers, "Guess what I dreamed last night."

"We don't care. Keep your dreams to yourself!" they answered.

Joseph told them anyway. "Last night," he said, "I dreamed that all of us were working together in the wheat field. The wheat was ripe, and we were cutting it and tying it into bundles. All of a sudden, my bundle stood straight up, and your bundles marched up and bowed down in front of mine."

"What a stupid dream!" they said. "Do you really think that someday you will be our master and we will be your servants?" They hated him even more for his dream, and they laughed at him, calling him "Your majesty, King Joseph!"

On another night, Joseph dreamed that the sun and the moon and eleven stars bowed down in front of him. Given the way his brothers reacted to his first dream, you would have thought that Joseph would have kept the next one to himself — but he didn't. When he told it to his brothers, they hated him more than ever. When he told it to his father Jacob, he didn't like it either.

"Joseph," he said, "you shouldn't talk like that! You're too proud. It's foolish for you to think that I and your mother and your brothers will ever bow down

before you!" But even though Jacob said this, he still wondered whether Joseph might become a mighty ruler someday.

Joseph's brothers also hated him because of the special coat that Jacob had given to him as a present. It was the most beautiful coat they had ever seen. None of the other brothers had ever received such a present, so they were both angry with their father and jealous of Joseph. "One of these days, we'll get even," they said. And sure enough, they did!

One morning soon after Joseph's seventeenth birthday, his father said to him, "Joseph, your brothers are over in the valley near the village of Shechem, taking care of the sheep. Take them this basket of food, find out how they're getting along, and then come back and tell me whether they're all right."

So Joseph started out toward Shechem, carrying the basket and wearing his

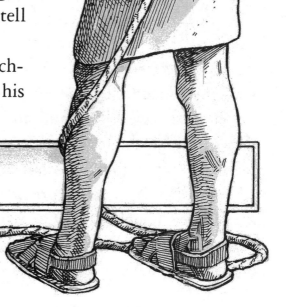

beautiful coat. But when his brothers saw him coming, one said, "Look who's coming — that high and mighty brother of ours. He thinks he's so much better than we are! Let's throw him into a pit and leave him there. That should put an end to his dreams!"

So they grabbed Joseph, pulled off his new coat, and threw him into a deep pit. Then they sat down to eat the food that Joseph had brought them. Later they looked up and saw a band of merchants with a train of camels coming toward them. The merchants were from the land of Midian and were on their way to Egypt to sell their spices and perfumes. This gave Joseph's brothers a new idea. "Let's sell him to the merchants," one said.

"Great!" said another. "That way we'll be rid of him without killing him!"

"And get some money besides!" said a third.

So they pulled Joseph up out of the pit and sold him to the merchants from Midian for twenty silver coins. But they kept Joseph's coat. As soon as the merchants were out of sight, they killed a goat, dipped the coat in the goat's blood, and took it back to their father.

"Look what we found!" they said. "This couldn't be Joseph's coat, could it?" Wasn't that a cruel thing to do!

Jacob recognized the coat and began to cry. "Yes, it is Joseph's coat," he sobbed. "I sent him to you with a basket of food. A lion or a bear must have killed him and dragged him away."

Thinking that Joseph was dead made Jacob so sad that he kept on weeping day after day. No one was able to comfort him.

"Joseph was so dear to me," he said. "As long as I live, I'll be sad because he's gone!"

In the meantime, the merchants arrived in Egypt with Joseph. They sold him as a slave to an Egyptian army officer by the name of Potiphar.

God was with Joseph, and Potiphar treated Joseph very kindly. Eventually he put him in charge of his whole household. Joseph knew God was with him, so he was happy even though he was far from home.

Prayer

Dear God, if I have more than some of my friends have, may I be grateful but not proud. If some of my friends have more than I have, may I be glad for them but not jealous. Make me happy with the things I have, ready to share, and never selfish, envious, or mean. In Jesus' name, amen.

Questions

1. Why did Joseph's brothers hate him? Was this partly Joseph's fault?
2. Did Joseph talk too much about his dreams?
3. How would you have felt if you were one of Joseph's brothers? How would you have treated him?
4. Which do you think was worse — what Joseph's brothers did to him or what they did to their father?
5. What can you do about pride and jealousy in your life?
6. What is your "dream" for the future? Is it a "dream" God would approve of?

Trapped in Prison

Genesis 39:20-23; 40:1-15, 20-23

I hope it will never happen to you, but how do you think you would feel if someone told a lie about you and, because of that lie, you were thrown into prison? On top of that, suppose this happened to you when you were far from home in a strange country with no family or friends to help you. What would you do? Would you say to yourself, "It doesn't pay to be good anymore," and give up?

Well, all this happened to Joseph. Do you suppose he gave up?

❦   ❦   ❦

"Good morning, my friend," said Joseph. "Why do you look so sad today?" Joseph was speaking to one of his fellow prisoners. His name was Pashah.

"I'm sad because of a strange dream I had last night," Pashah answered, "and because I can't find anyone to tell me what it means."

"Maybe I can help you," said Joseph. "Dreams come from God.

[22]

Tell me your dream, and I will pray to him to reveal its meaning to us."

Now Pashah had once been chief butler to Pharaoh, the king of Egypt. Every day he had served the king his meals in the palace. But one day he did something that Pharaoh didn't like, so the king ordered him thrown into prison. There he and Joseph became good friends.

But why was Joseph in prison? Not because he had done something wrong, but because someone had told a lie about him when he was a slave in the house of Potiphar. Potiphar was the Egyptian army officer who had bought Joseph from the Midianite merchants after he had been sold to them by his brothers. It was Potiphar's wife who told the lie: she claimed that Joseph had insulted her. Since Joseph was only a slave, he wasn't given a trial. Potiphar simply threw him into prison.

But Joseph didn't allow himself to become discouraged. He still trusted God. Also, he did everything he could to help and cheer up the other prisoners. Because of this, they all liked him, and before long the warden of the prison put him in charge of all the other prisoners.

But back to Pashah. This is the dream he told Joseph: "In my dream I was standing beside a vine that had three branches. Suddenly, buds appeared on the vine, then blossoms, then bunches of ripe grapes. I had Pharaoh's cup in my hand. I took the grapes, squeezed their juice into the cup, and gave it to Pharaoh."

After Joseph had prayed to God for wisdom, he turned to Pashah and said, "This is the meaning of your dream. The three branches of the vine stand for three days. In three days Pharaoh will send for you to come to the palace. You will be his butler again and will serve him food and wine as you used to do."

Then Pashah was no longer sad, but very happy. "Joseph, you are truly a wonderful friend," he said. "I wish there were something I could do to show you how grateful I am!"

"There *is* something you can do for me," replied Joseph. "You remember, as I once told you, that I was sold by my brothers and carried away from my home. Also, in my master Potiphar's house, I

did nothing wrong — I don't deserve to be in prison. When you go back to the palace, tell the king about me and ask him to set me free."

Pashah promised to help Joseph, but when he was restored to his place in the palace, he was so busy with his duties and so lost in his own happiness that he forgot his promise. In fact, it was two whole years before he even remembered Joseph. Pashah was not really very grateful, was he? Grateful people remember those who do kind things for them. Remember that the next time someone is kind to you.

Prayer

Dear God, help me not to give up when I feel blue. When I am discouraged, may I remember this is the time, above all other times, to be brave.

Teach me, too, that when I help others, as Joseph did, I make my own troubles much lighter. And help me to remember those who are kind to me so I can thank them. In Jesus' name, amen.

Questions

1. What are some of the "wrong" things Joseph could have done while he was in prison?
2. What were the "right" things he did do?

3. What do you think would have happened to Joseph if he had been angry and mean as a prisoner?

4. If someone told a lie about you or blamed you for something that wasn't your fault, what would you do?

5. Pashah broke his promise to Joseph. How do you feel about people who break their promises to you?

6. Can you think of any promises you may have forgotten? Promises you made to God? to a member of your family? to a friend?

7. What should you do about the promises you have forgotten?

From Prison to Palace

Genesis 41

What is the most wonderful surprise you ever got? Was it a surprise that someone planned for you? Was it just luck? Or was it something God did for you? Was your surprise something for you alone, or were you able to share it with someone else?

❧   ❧   ❧

Pharaoh, the king of Egypt, got up early. He paced the floor of his room, deep in thought. He called together his wise men and talked with them for some time. After they left, the king was still pacing.

When Pashah, the king's butler, brought in Pharaoh's breakfast, he could tell the king was troubled. "Why is my lord so worried this morning?" he asked.

"I hardly slept at all last night," replied the king. "I had two strange dreams, and I have no idea what they mean. Already I have called in my wise men and magicians, but none of them can explain the dreams to me."

Then Pashah remembered a promise he had made two years earlier. He felt very sorry that he had not remembered it sooner. He had promised to tell the king about Joseph, who was in prison for no good reason.

"My lord," he said, "when I was in prison, I had a dream that troubled me. Another prisoner was there, a wonderful young man named Joseph. I told him my dream, and he was able to tell me what it meant. Perhaps he could do the same for you."

"Send for him at once!" ordered Pharaoh.

Joseph was hastily removed from prison. Before meeting with Pharaoh, he took time first to shave and bathe and put on fresh clothes. Then, looking his best, he went in and stood before the king.

Pharaoh said to him, "Last night I had two dreams that

have been troubling me. My butler tells me that you are able to explain the meaning of dreams. Is this true?"

"The power is not in me," Joseph replied, "but in God. Let the king tell his dreams to me, and God will give us the answer."

"In my first dream," Pharaoh said, "I was standing beside the Nile River. Out of the water came seven cows that were fat and healthy-looking, and they began to eat grass in the meadow. After that, seven other cows came out of the river — thin and bony. I have never seen such thin cows in all my life — at least, not in Egypt! Then the seven thin cows ate up the seven fat ones. But afterward they were still as thin and bony as they were before. The dream upset me and woke me up.

"After a while, I fell asleep and dreamed again. In my second dream, I saw seven ears of corn — large and plump — all growing on one stalk. On another stalk were seven lean ears — withered, thin, and small. While I was looking, the seven thin ears ate up the seven good ears.

"I have told these dreams to my wise men and magicians, but they haven't been able to explain their meaning."

Then Joseph said to the king, "God is telling Pharaoh what he is about to do. The two dreams mean the same thing. The seven fat cows and the seven large ears of corn stand for the seven years that the land of Egypt will have good crops and plenty of food. After these will come seven years of hunger and famine, when the crops will fail and there will be great suffering.

"God is showing this to you so that you can prepare for the famine and save your people. So I urge the king to find a man who is both wise and good and make him governor over all the land of Egypt. Let this man have officers under him who will gather, during the seven years of plenty, large supplies of grain and put them in great storehouses in the cities.

Then, when the years of famine come, there will be food to keep the people from starving."

Then Pharaoh said to his servants and court officers, "Where could we find anyone wiser and better than this man who has told us these things?" Turning to Joseph, he said, "Since the spirit of God is in you, and since he has made known all these things to you, you shall be governor over the land of Egypt. You shall be in charge of gathering and storing up the grain before the years of famine."

Then the king took off his ring and put it on Joseph's finger, and he ordered that Joseph should be dressed in beautiful clothes, with a chain of gold around his neck. Pharaoh also had Joseph ride through the streets in a chariot behind his own, and all the people bowed before him. In this way God brought Joseph out of prison and made him governor over all the land of Egypt. All this was part of God's wonderful plan!

During the seven years of plenty, Joseph stored up huge amounts of grain. When the famine came, he sold the stored grain to the people of Egypt and also to people from neighboring lands. By doing this he was able to save thousands of people from starving. Even his own family, including the brothers who had sold him into Egypt, might have starved if it hadn't been for Joseph and what he was able to do for them.

Prayer

Dear God, when something good happens to me, may I remember it is because you love me. May I be grateful but not proud. Then may I show my gratitude by doing things that will help others, just as Joseph did. In Jesus' name, amen.

Questions

1. Joseph had to be very patient during the two years that the butler forgot about him. Do you have patience with God's plans for you?
2. How was Joseph able to explain dreams?
3. How does God help you in the things you are called upon to do?
4. Do you think everything you have is a gift from God? See 1 Corinthians 4:7. How should you treat these "gifts"?
5. Why did Pharaoh believe that Joseph would make a good governor? Should Christians make better workers and officials than people who are not Christians?
6. If Joseph were here today, what do you think he would do about the starving people in the world?
7. What should we do about world hunger? What can you do about it?
8. Do you think it's wrong to eat too much or to waste food? Why?

From Feast to Famine

Genesis 42

Isn't it amazing how some people are able to hide the bad things they do? They may cheat at school, steal from a store, rob a bank, or even kill someone, and they are never found out.

But there's a verse in the Bible that says, "Be sure your sin will find you out" (Numbers 32:23). This means that while we may be able to hide our sins from others, we cannot hide them from God or ourselves. When we do something wrong, the memory of it follows us like our shadow everywhere we go. Our conscience won't let us forget it, and we will always be troubled by it unless we do what we should to correct the wrong. And that was just the problem Joseph's brothers had.

❦   ❦   ❦

Soon after Joseph was made governor of Egypt, Pharaoh's dream began to come true. All over the land, the fields brought forth big harvests. And Joseph, wise governor that he was, lost no time in buying up the surplus grain and storing it in great barns which he had built in the cities. For seven years he did this. Then the seven years of famine began, and the people of Egypt came to buy back the grain they had sold to Joseph. Since the famine struck other countries too, people came to Egypt from far away to buy grain.

Joseph's father, Jacob, and his family still lived in Canaan, where the famine took its toll. One day Jacob said to his sons, "Why do you look so worried? Although our grain is almost gone, I have heard that there is plenty in Egypt. Saddle the donkeys and go down and buy some for us. If we do nothing, we will starve." So ten of Joseph's sons, each riding a donkey, set out for Egypt, which was a long journey away. But Benjamin, the youngest, stayed with Jacob.

Now Joseph and Benjamin were "full" brothers; they had the same father and the same mother. Her name was Rachel, but she was no longer living; she was the wife that Jacob had loved the most. The other ten brothers were half brothers to Joseph and Benjamin — Jacob was their father, but they had different mothers. This explains why Joseph always felt closer to Benjamin than to any of his other brothers. It also explains why Jacob wanted Benjamin, his youngest son, to stay with him. He had already lost Joseph, and he didn't want to lose Benjamin.

Some days later, Joseph's ten half-brothers arrived in Egypt, asked where they could buy grain, and were sent to the governor's office. Now when they had sold Joseph as a slave some fifteen years earlier, they had never dreamed he would one day become governor. Besides, he had been a boy then; he was a man now. So, although Joseph recognized his brothers, none of them recognized him.

As they bowed before him with their faces to the ground, Joseph wondered whether they were still as selfish and cruel as they had been on the day they had thrown him into the pit and sold him, or whether they had changed and were now good, kind, and honest. He decided to test them. So instead of telling them who he was and speaking kindly to them, he said in a stern voice, "You are spies! You've come to see what our country is like. Then you'll go back and tell our enemies."

"No, my lord," they answered. "We aren't spies — we're honest men. Everything we've told you is the truth. We're brothers, all the sons of one man in the land of Canaan. We've come to Egypt for only one purpose. Our father Jacob sent us to buy grain because of the famine."

"Do you have any other brothers?" Joseph asked.

"Yes, two others," they answered. "One, whose name was Joseph, is dead. The youngest one, whose name is Benjamin, is with our father back in Canaan."

"You say you're telling the truth?" replied Joseph. "You say you have a younger brother? Then you must prove it! One of you may take the grain you need back home. The rest of you will stay here as my prisoners. You will be set free only if your youngest brother is brought to Egypt. I must see him with my own eyes! Then I'll believe you." Then Joseph put them all in prison for three days.

On the third day, Joseph pretended to have changed his mind. "I will keep only one of you," he said. "The rest of you may return home with grain. But you must bring your youngest brother back with you to prove you aren't lying."

At this point, Joseph's brothers turned and began talking with one another in Hebrew, thinking that Joseph couldn't understand what they were saying. They thought he was an Egyptian because he had used an interpreter (a man who spoke both Hebrew and Egyptian) to talk to them. But Joseph heard and understood every word.

"All this has happened because of what we did to our brother Joseph years ago," said one.

"Our sin has found us out," another added.

"I remember how he cried, stretched out his hands, and begged us not to sell him," a third said.

"Yes," said Reuben, the oldest, "and I pleaded with you not to harm him, but you wouldn't listen. Now God is punishing us!"

As Joseph listened, he couldn't keep back his tears. He walked out of the room so his brothers wouldn't see him crying. He saw they were changing, and so great was his love for them that he wanted to forgive them then and there. But he decided it was best to go ahead with the test.

So he came back and ordered Simeon, the second oldest brother, to be put in prison. "He will be set free," said Joseph, "only if you prove you have told me the truth by bringing your youngest brother to Egypt. Unless you bring him, I won't sell you any more grain."

So the other brothers loaded their sacks, which Joseph's servants had filled with grain, onto their donkeys and started back to Canaan.

When they stopped for the first night, they made an amazing discovery. When they opened their sacks, every one of them discovered in the top of his sack the bag of money he had used to pay for his grain!

When they saw this, they were amazed and also afraid. Of course, none of them knew that Joseph had ordered his servants to put the money there after they filled the sacks.

When they arrived home, they told their father all that had happened in Egypt — how the governor had accused them of being spies and of telling lies and had said he wouldn't sell them any more grain or set their brother Simeon free unless they brought Benjamin back with them.

They didn't know that all of this trouble would turn out well. But they had learned how wicked they had been to sell Joseph as a slave. They were now beginning to listen to their conscience — and all of this points to a happy ending.

Prayer

Dear God, when I do something that makes me feel bad inside, may I know that it is because my conscience is telling me what I did was wrong. Then help me to do what my conscience tells me I should do to set the wrong right, so I may feel right inside again. In Jesus' name, amen.

Questions

1. How did Joseph prepare for the famine?
2. Why did Joseph feel closer to Benjamin than to the other brothers?
3. If your brothers had treated you the way Joseph's brothers treated him, how would you feel if they came to you for help? What would you do?
4. How did Joseph feel about his brothers when they came to him? What did he wonder about them?
5. How did Joseph test his brothers?
6. Do you think Joseph was fair to them? Why or why not?
7. When you've done something wrong, how do you feel inside?
8. What should you do to set the wrong right, and when should you do it?

Dinner at the Governor's House

Genesis 43

Suppose you had had a bad day at school — someone shoved you as you were coming down the steps, or someone said something mean about you or laughed at you when you made a mistake. How would you feel about going back the next day?

You wouldn't want to go, would you? You would be tempted to say you had a headache and stay home. But deep down you would know that you had to go back. You couldn't get an education if you stayed away. So, even though you would dread it, you would go back. And later you would be glad you did.

❧   ❧   ❧

It was time for Jacob's sons to go back to Egypt for more grain, but they didn't want to go. They were afraid because of the way they had been treated the first time. They wondered what the governor would say about the money they had found in their sacks. They wondered if their brother Simeon, whom the governor had put in prison, was still alive. These were some of the reasons they didn't want to go back.

But their supply of grain was almost gone and the famine was still very severe. Only in Egypt could they buy grain. So one morning Jacob said to his sons, "You'll have to go back to Egypt and buy us some more grain."

"Then we'll have to take Benjamin with us," said Judah.

"No. He's my youngest son. I've told you before: he will stay with me. I can't do without him," Jacob replied.

"Then there's no point in our going back," Judah said. "The governor told us over and over that he wouldn't even see us unless we brought Benjamin with us."

"But why did you tell him you had another brother?" asked Jacob.

"He wanted to know all about our family," Judah answered. "'Is your father still alive? Do you have another brother?' he asked. We had no way of knowing that he would say, 'You must bring your youngest brother with you the next time you come.' But he really meant it. That's the reason he wouldn't let Simeon come back with us."

"What am I going to do?" said Jacob. "Joseph is dead. And Simeon may be dead, too. I can't bear to lose Benjamin, my youngest son." Now Jacob was the one reluctant about the trip.

Judah laid his hand on his father's shoulder and said, "Listen, Father. Put him in my care. I give you my solemn promise that I will see that no harm comes to him and that we'll bring him back. But we have to have grain. Let us go before we starve."

So Jacob gave in. "I suppose there's nothing else to do," he said. "But take with you a present of fruit and honey and nuts for the governor, and also take extra money so that you can return what was found in your bags. And may God give the governor a tender heart, so that he may set Simeon free and send Benjamin back."

So Jacob's sons set out again for the land of Egypt. A number of days later, they arrived at the governor's office. When Joseph was told that they had come back and that their youngest brother was with them,

he said to his chief officer, "Bring them to my house and prepare your best dinner for them."

But when Judah and his brothers heard they were to be brought to the governor's house, they were afraid and said to each other, "It's because of the money we found in our sacks. The governor is going to throw us into prison with Simeon."

So they told the governor's chief officer about the money and offered to give it back. But he wouldn't take it. "You don't owe anything," he said. "I myself remember you paid your bill in full when you were here before. God must have put the money in your sacks."

Then he brought out Simeon and took all of the brothers to the governor's house. Soon the governor came in, and the brothers bowed and offered the presents of fruit and honey and nuts they had brought. Joseph thanked them, then asked, "How is your father, the old man about whom you told me before?"

"Our father is still alive and is well," they answered.

Then, seeing Benjamin, his youngest brother whom he loved so dearly, Joseph said, "And this, I take it, is your youngest brother, whom you told me about?" Turning to Benjamin, he added, "May God bless you, my son."

At this point, Joseph hurriedly left the room. So great was the love he felt for Benjamin that he couldn't keep from crying. As soon as he had dried his tears and washed his face, he came back. "Let dinner be served," he said to his servants, and he led his brothers to the table. They were amazed to find their places had been arranged in the order of their ages — from Reuben, the oldest, down to Benjamin, the youngest. They couldn't understand how the governor knew their ages! But they did know it was very special to be having dinner at his house. So, as they sat at the table eating and drinking, they forgot their fears and had a good time together.

Prayer

Dear God, keep me from expecting life to be pleasant all of the time. Every day I'm called upon to do things that I don't like to do. But help me to do them anyway even when they're hard, when I know I should! May I do what is right just because it is right. In Jesus' name, amen.

Questions

1. Why didn't Jacob's sons want to go back to Egypt?
2. Why did they have to go? Why did Benjamin have to go along?
3. How did Jacob feel about letting Benjamin go?
4. How do you think Benjamin felt about going to Egypt?
5. Could you make someone a promise like the one Judah made to his father? Why might you do it?
6. Why did Joseph leave the room after he had greeted Benjamin? How do you suppose his brothers felt? What might they have guessed to be the possible reasons for his leaving?
7. What does the word "duty" mean to you?
8. What duties do you have?
9. How should you perform them? Do you? Will you?

Missing —
The Governor's Cup!

Genesis 44–45

Suppose you felt very sad inside because of some wrong you had done to a member of your family or a dear friend. You knew you were guilty and hadn't been forgiven. You'd feel pretty bad, wouldn't you?

Then suppose that, all of a sudden, all that changed! You said you were sorry, and you were forgiven. Wouldn't that be a wonderful feeling?

❦   ❦   ❦

On the day that Joseph had his brothers for dinner in his house, he watched how they acted toward each other. He was almost sure they were now kind and good and no longer mean and cruel as they had been when they sold him into Egypt. But the next morning he decided to put them to one more test.

Calling to his chief officer, he said, "Fill their sacks with grain, and again, put every man's money in the mouth of his sack and tie it tight. And in the top of the sack of the youngest also put my *silver cup!*"

The officer did as he was told, and soon afterward Joseph's brothers rode away, each with a sack of grain. They had gone only a little way when Joseph said to his officer, "Hurry! Go after the men and ask them why they have given evil for good by stealing my silver cup."

The officer soon caught up with them and ordered them to stop. "You're thieves!" he accused them. "The governor was so good to you, and you've repaid his kindness by stealing his silver cup!"

"We aren't thieves — we're honest men!" they answered. "Don't you remember how we brought back the money we found in our sacks when we bought this second supply of grain? We have stolen nothing. Search our sacks, and if you find the cup, all of us will become your master's slaves."

Quickly each brother opened his sack. The officer began his search with the oldest brother's sack, and looked in Benjamin's sack last. In each man's sack was his money, and in Benjamin's sack the officer found Joseph's silver cup!

Heartsick, the brothers hurried back to Joseph's house. They bowed before him, terribly afraid. Then Judah said, "My lord, we don't know what to say. We are ready to become your slaves, we along with our youngest brother, in whose sack your cup was found."

"No," said Joseph. "Only he shall be my slave. The rest of you, go on home to your father!"

Then Judah, remembering his promise to his father, came close to Joseph and said, "O my lord, our father is an old man. Benjamin is his youngest son, and he loves him very dearly. If we go back without him, my father will die. My lord, before we left to come back to Egypt, I promised my father that I would see that no harm came to Benjamin and that I would surely bring him back. So I plead with you, let me stay as your slave, my lord, but let the boy go back with his brothers, so that our father's heart may not be broken."

At this point Joseph could keep his secret no longer. He dismissed his servants, then broke down and cried. He said, "I am Joseph your brother. Don't be afraid. I have only been testing you. And I know that you are now kind and good men who are loyal to each other. I have forgiven you, and God has made everything turn out for good. He has made me governor over all the land of Egypt, and through me he has saved your lives and the lives of many others during this time of famine."

Then Joseph took Benjamin into his arms, and the two brothers laughed and cried as they hugged one another. Next Joseph kissed all his brothers, and they laughed and cried too — both for sorrow and for joy!

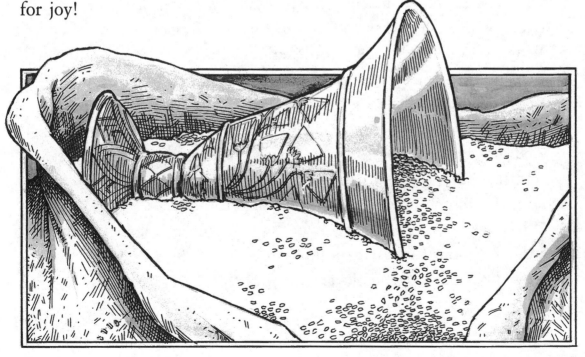

Prayer

Dear God, how I hate that bad feeling inside of me when I've done something wrong! I do thank you that there's a way to get rid of that feeling. Whenever I do or say something I shouldn't to a friend or a member of my family, help me to say "I'm sorry" and ask to be forgiven. Help me to show my love for my family and my friends by always being loyal and doing everything I can to make them happy. In Jesus' name, amen.

Questions

1. Why did Joseph "test" his brothers? How did he test them?
2. Do you feel different about Joseph's brothers after Joseph's tests than you did when they sold him? Why or why not?
3. Why do you think Joseph ordered his silver cup to be put in Benjamin's sack instead of in the sack of one of the older brothers?
4. Why did Judah offer to save Benjamin?
5. Why did God allow Joseph to be sold into Egypt? Do you feel that God also has a purpose in the things that happen to you? (See Romans 8:28.)
6. How did Joseph prove he still loved his brothers?
7. What does it mean to you to be loyal to the members of your family? to your friends? to Jesus?
8. How did Jesus prove his loyalty to you? (See John 15:13.)

Family Reunion

Genesis 45–47:12

When we're young, perhaps we think too much about what we want our parents to do for us, and not enough about what we can and should do for them. Sometimes we may even feel a little ashamed of them because they don't dress as well or make as much money or have as good an education as the parents of some of our friends.

In Joseph's day, Egyptians thought shepherds were not as good as other people. But, far from being ashamed of his shepherd father, Joseph did something that showed he not only loved him but was proud of him, too.

❧   ❧   ❧

One of the first things Joseph had done when he revealed his identity to his brothers and told them he had forgiven them was to ask about Jacob. "And how is my father? Is he still alive and well?"

"He is alive and well," they answered, "but he is now an old man and growing feeble."

"You must hurry back to him and tell him that God has made me governor over all the land of Egypt," said Joseph. "You must bring him here to be near me so that I can take care of him, because the famine will last for five more years. You too must move to Egypt, my dear brothers," Joseph continued. "Bring your wives and children and all your possessions. Here you may care for your flocks and herds. I will look after you, and you will be safe from all fear of the famine."

So Joseph's brothers left with food and wagons he supplied them with to bring their families back to Egypt. Not many days later, they arrived back home. Running to their father's tent, they shouted, "Joseph is still alive! He is governor over all the land of Egypt!" At first Jacob couldn't believe them. He almost fainted. The news was just too good to be true. But when they told Jacob everything Joseph had said and showed him the wagons and the food he had sent, joy came over the old man's face, and he said, "Say no more — I believe you! My son Joseph is alive; I will go see him before I die." So Jacob told his sons to fold their tents, pack their belongings, and gather their flocks and herds. A few days later, they were on their way to Egypt.

When they arrived, Joseph went to the palace and said to Pharaoh, "My father and my brothers with their families are here. They are shepherds, so they have brought their flocks and their herds with them." From among his eleven brothers Joseph chose five of them and presented them to Pharaoh.

Then Pharaoh said to Joseph, "The country of Egypt is before you. Settle them on the best of the land. Let them dwell in the land of Goshen. And put some of the men in charge of my cattle."

Now, of course, Joseph knew how the Egyptians felt about shepherds. They thought shepherds weren't as good as everyone else. Still, he was proud of his father and took him to the palace and introduced him to Pharaoh.

Pharaoh spoke kindly to Jacob, then asked, "How old are you?"

"One hundred and thirty years old," Jacob replied, "and my life has been full of trouble, because for so long I thought my son Joseph was dead."

"But now you see he is very much alive, and governor over all the land, second only to me!" Pharaoh replied. Then he added, "You and your sons are welcome. I have told the governor to allow you to settle in the best part of Egypt. The land of Goshen will be your home. There your sons will find good pastures for their flocks and herds and no danger of famine."

"The king is most kind," said Jacob. Then, as he and Joseph were leaving, he asked God to bless Pharaoh.

Thus it came about that Jacob was united again with his long-lost son. For many years, he and his other sons and their families lived happily together in the land of Egypt under the loving care of Joseph, who continued to be the governor, second only to the king.

Prayer

Dear God, help me to be as unselfish and forgiving and as kind and helpful to all members of my family as Joseph was to his brothers and his father. In Jesus' name, amen.

Questions

1. What message did Joseph send to his father?
2. What finally convinced Jacob that Joseph was still alive?

3. Why do you think Pharaoh was glad when he heard that Joseph's brothers and father were in Egypt? What did he say?

4. If you had been Joseph, would you have introduced your father to Pharaoh? Why or why not?

5. What were some of the things that made Jacob and his sons happy as they continued to live in the land of Egypt? Do you think they might have been homesick for Canaan sometimes?

6. Name ways you can be helpful to older people.

7. What does the Bible teach about how you should treat your father and mother? (See Ephesians 6:1-2.)

Cradle in the River

Exodus 2:1-10

When you were a little baby, how many hours every day do you suppose your mother spent taking care of you? And did anyone pay her to do it? Of course not! She did it just because she loved you! But did you know that there's a story in the Bible about a mother who really did get paid for taking care of her own baby? Her name was Jochebed.

Four hundred years had passed since Jacob and his sons and their families had moved to Egypt. Since that time, other kings, also called Pharaoh, had come to the throne. They didn't remember Joseph and the promise the king had made about providing for Joseph's relatives. And all of Jacob's descendants, called Hebrews, or the people of Israel, had been made slaves.

🦎 🦎 🦎

"Miriam," said Jochebed, "you've been so good to help me take care of your baby brother ever since he was born, but now he's three months old, and I'm afraid we can't keep him in the house any longer."

Miriam was confused. "What do you mean, Mother?" she asked. "Isn't he safe here with us?"

"No, my dear, he isn't safe. Pharaoh, the king, has given an order that every Hebrew baby boy shall be thrown into the river. Every day I'm afraid his soldiers may come and search our house. You see, Miriam," Jochebed went on to explain, "Pharaoh is afraid that if our boys should live and grow up, they will become strong and brave men who will fight and win freedom for our people. That's the reason he's ordered all Hebrew baby boys to be drowned."

"Oh, Mother, what are we going to do?"

"I have a plan," said Jochebed, "and I need you to help me."

Then she sent Miriam down to the river to gather and bring back an armful of the tall reeds that grew along the bank. Together they wove the reeds into a basket about the size and shape of a baby's cradle. Next they lined and sealed it with tar and pitch. When it was finished and dried, what do you suppose they had? A cradle that was also a little boat!

The next morning, they put the baby into the little boat and hid him in the tall reeds beside the river. While Jochebed went back to her duties in the house, Miriam stayed nearby to watch, so no harm could come to her little brother.

Before long, Miriam saw the Egyptian princess, with her maidens, coming down to the river to bathe! What should she do? Should she run and call her mother? If she did, the princess and her maidens might find the baby and carry him away before Miriam and her mother could get back. They might even throw him into the river, as the king had ordered! So Miriam stayed.

As she waited, she hoped the princess and her maidens wouldn't see the little boat hidden in the reeds. But they did, and soon they were very close to it. The princess stopped and, pointing toward it, asked one of her maidens to bring it to her.

Then Miriam ran as fast as her feet could carry her down the path toward them. By the time she arrived, the princess had the basket in her hands. "What a darling baby!" she said. "This must be one of the Hebrew children." Her maidens said nothing, waiting to see what the princess would do. You see, she was the daughter of the king who had given the cruel order. Miriam waited, too. Then the baby began to cry! His tears came just at the right time. They touched the heart of the princess, and she took him out of the basket and held him in her arms.

"You dear little baby!" she said. "Shh, shh, don't you cry! No one is ever going to harm you. I'm going to take you to the palace to be my own son. And your name will be Moses because we found you in the river" (*Moses* means "drawn out of the water").

Then Miriam approached the princess. Bowing low, she said, "Would it please the princess if I find her a nurse from among the Hebrew women to care for the baby?"

"Yes, my dear," replied the princess. "I shall most certainly need a nurse."

"My mother is the best nurse in the world!" said Miriam. "If you can wait for just a moment, I will bring her."

Then up the path she ran, straight to her home. "Mother, Mother!" she shouted as she pushed open the door. "Come right away! The princess sent me to bring you."

As they hurried down to the river, she told her mother the whole story. When the princess saw Jochebed, she was very pleased. "I found this baby in this little basket in the reeds by the riverbank," she said. "Would you be willing to be his nurse? I will pay you well."

"But I couldn't leave my family," said Jochebed. So the princess agreed to let Jochebed keep Moses in her own home until he was older.

Later Moses was brought to the palace and treated as if he were the son of the princess. There he went to the royal school, received a wonderful education, and became a very great man. But great and famous though he became, Moses never forgot his wonderful mother and his brave sister and how they had saved his life when he was a baby.

The Bible doesn't tell us how much the princess paid Jochebed for taking care of her own baby. But we can be sure that no amount of

money could compare with the joy that was hers as she watched her little son grow up and in time become such a noble man. That has always been, and still is, a good mother's greatest reward!

Prayer

Dear God, I thank you for those who took care of me so lovingly when I was too little to take care of myself and for the way they still love me. May I never disappoint those who have done so much for me, who believe the best about me, and who expect the best from me. In Jesus' name, amen.

Questions

1. Why was Jochebed's baby not safe at home?
2. Do you think Jochebed was a good mother? Why?
3. How do you think Jochebed felt about having the princess "adopt" her son?
4. What reasons can you find for liking Miriam?
5. Can you think of ways you and your mother or father can get along with each other and work together as well as Miriam and Jochebed did?
6. In what ways can you thank your parents for what they do for you?

Mystery in the Desert!

Exodus 2:11–4

Suppose that you were very rich. Imagine, too, that you owned a factory not far from your home. All the people in the factory had to work very hard and for long hours but for very low wages, so they were very poor. And their bosses didn't treat them well. Suppose one thing more — that among the poor people working in the factory were your father and mother and certain other members of your family.

Knowing all this, how would you feel? Would you be content to go on living for yourself in your beautiful home, thinking only of your own happiness? Or would you be very unhappy, troubled about your mother and father and the other people in the factory? Would you want to do something that would change things? What do you feel God would want you to do?

Your answer to these questions should help you to understand how Moses felt.

❧   ❧   ❧

When Moses became a man, he wasn't happy as a prince because his own people, the Hebrews, were slaves to the Egyptians.

He was both sad and angry as he saw what their cruel masters did to them and how much they suffered. The slaves had to make bricks out of mud and straw, and they were often beaten because they didn't make them fast enough. One day Moses saw an Egyptian beating a Hebrew with a club. It looked like the Hebrew was going to be killed, so Moses rushed to his rescue. Seeing no one else around, Moses killed the Egyptian and hid his body in the sand.

The next day Moses tried to break up a fight between two Hebrews. But one of them, the one who had started the fight, said, "Who made you our judge? Are you going to kill me the way you killed the Egyptian yesterday?" When Moses heard that, he was afraid. He had hoped no one would find out about the Egyptian. But soon even Pharaoh knew about it, and he ordered his police to find Moses and kill him.

Moses was afraid to stay in Egypt, so he went away to a land called Midian. There he sat down by a well. Soon seven sisters came to water their father's sheep, but some shepherds also came and drove the women away so they could water their own sheep first. Again, Moses came to the rescue. Then he watered the sisters' sheep himself. The women were grateful and told their father, Jethro, about Moses. Jethro invited Moses to live with them, and eventually Moses married one of Jethro's daughters.

One day, as Moses was watching Jethro's sheep in a desert place close to a mountain called Horeb, he saw a very strange sight. A bush was on fire, but it didn't burn up! It just kept on burning!

Moses said to himself, "I'll go up closer to see this strange sight." As he came closer, he heard a voice calling his name. God was calling to him out of the bush.

The voice said, "Moses, I have seen the suffering of my people in the land of Egypt and have heard their cry because their masters are so cruel. I am going to deliver them from their slavery and bring them into a new land, a good land, where they may live in freedom and may worship and serve me as I shall command them."

Then the voice spoke again: "Moses, I have chosen *you* to deliver my people. I am going to send you to Pharaoh. You will tell him he must set my people free. Then you will lead them out of the land of Egypt and bring them into the new land that I will give them."

"But I can't go to Pharaoh!" Moses replied. "He won't listen to me."

"I will be with you to help you and give you courage," God answered. "And I will give you power to work great signs and wonders until Pharaoh will let the people go. Then you will come and worship me upon this mountain."

"What if the Israelites say, 'Who sent you?'" Moses asked. "When I say, 'The God of your fathers has sent me,' what if they say, 'What is his name?' What will I tell them?"

"I am who I am," God answered. "Tell them that 'I AM' sent you. Tell them I am the God of Abraham, Isaac, and Jacob."

"But what if they don't believe me?" Moses argued.

God answered, "What's that in your hand, Moses?"

"What, this?" said Moses. "Well, it's my rod — my shepherd's rod."

"Throw it down."

When Moses threw it down, it became a snake, and Moses ran from it. But the Lord called him back. "Now pick it up — by the tail." Moses reached for the snake. It turned and looked at him; then it began to hiss. Moses was nervous, but he obeyed. As soon as he took hold of the snake, it became a rod again. God gave Moses the power to work other signs, too.

Still Moses made excuses. "But I can't speak well," he said. "I wouldn't know what to say to the king."

But God said, "Who made your mouth, Moses? I did. And I can put words in it for you. Now, go. I am with you to help you."

Still Moses held back. "My Lord," he said, "I just can't do it. Please send someone else."

Then the Lord became angry. "Take Aaron your brother with you," he said. "He's a good speaker. Through you I will tell him what to say. Together you will go to Pharaoh and tell him to set my people free.

At first Pharaoh will say no. But because of the miracles I will work through you, he will change his mind."

So, with God guiding and helping him, Moses went back to the land of Egypt. There he did become the great leader of his people. Later, they did come to Mount Horeb, sometimes called Sinai, to the very same place where God had called Moses. There the people camped for several weeks to worship God and to thank him for their new freedom. And there Moses received God's law, known today as the Ten Commandments, to help God's people to live for him.

Prayer

Dear God, I want my life to count someday for something fine and good. I believe you will help me, even as you helped Moses. Thank you for the Bible, which teaches me how to live for you and make my life count. May I listen and obey, as Moses did. In Jesus' name, amen.

Questions

1. Why wasn't Moses happy as a prince in Pharaoh's palace?
2. How do you feel when you hear about people who aren't treated well, who are hungry and homeless? What can you do to help them?

3. Why did Moses leave Egypt?

4. What strange sight did he see in the desert one day?

5. What did God want Moses to do?

6. What do you think of someone who says, "It's my life, and I have the right to do what I want with it"?

7. What do you think God meant when he said, "I am who I am"?

8. How can you find out what God wants you to do with your life?

9. How many of the Ten Commandments do you know? Recite as many as you can.

Giants and Grasshoppers
Numbers 13–14; Joshua 1:1-9

Suppose for some good reason you needed to go through a dark forest at night. Suppose it was cloudy, so you couldn't see the moon or even the stars. Would you be afraid? Would you say, "I can't do it"?

Then suppose your father were to say, "I'll go with you." Would you still be afraid? Would you still say, "I can't do it"? Fear isn't a bad thing in and of itself. But sometimes it makes us cowards when we should be brave.

There was a time when God's people were like that. They were cowards at heart and listened to the voice of fear rather than to the voice of faith.

❧   ❧   ❧

The people of Israel had almost reached Canaan, the land God had promised them in Egypt. You will remember that they were led out of Egypt toward this new land by God's brave servant, Moses, and his

brother, Aaron. For over a year, they had been moving toward it through a wild desert country where food was scarce and life was hard. But now, at last, they were close to Canaan.

Before they went into Canaan, God told Moses to send some men ahead to see what it was like. Moses chose twelve men, called scouts, to do this.

As they set out, Moses said to them, "Go and find out what the land is like, whether it's rich or poor, whether it's hilly or flat, whether it has few trees or many trees. Also find out what the people are like. See whether they are strong or weak, few or many, and see how they live, whether they group together in tents or live in walled cities. Bring back some of the fruits of the land, too, so that we may taste them. Be brave and bring back a true report."

The twelve scouts set out as Moses had commanded. They passed by several cities, which were big and well protected, and where they saw men who were very tall and strong. They also went through fertile valleys in which the vines were loaded with ripe grapes. They cut one big bunch of grapes to bring back with them. It was so large that two men carried it between them on a long pole resting on their shoulders. They took some pomegranates and figs to bring back too.

Forty days later, the scouts returned, and Moses and all the people gathered together to hear what they had to say. Now, of course, all twelve scouts had seen exactly the same things — the people of Canaan and their houses, their cities, their fields, and their vineyards. The only difference was that two of them, Joshua and Caleb, were men of courage and faith. The other ten were not.

The ten said, "The land is rich and fruitful, and there is plenty of milk and honey. But the cities are like forts, and the people are too strong — they're like giants. Compared to them, we're like grasshoppers. We can't take the land."

But Joshua and Caleb said, "Don't lose faith in God or be afraid. If God is pleased with us, he will bring us into the land and will help us to take it."

The sad part of the story is that the people listened to the ten men, not to Joshua and Caleb. They grumbled and complained to Moses and Aaron. "It would have been better if we had stayed in Egypt," they said. "Why did you bring us out here to this desert, where we may be killed by those giants in Canaan?"

So the people refused to go up and take the land, and in the end they paid a big price for being cowards and complainers. For forty more years God let them wander in the desert country. There they suffered many more hardships and trials before he finally gave them the land as he had promised.

By that time, only two of the twelve scouts were still living. Can you guess which two they were? Yes, Joshua and Caleb, the two brave ones! That was the way God rewarded them for their courage — he kept them strong and well so they were able to march into Canaan and help his people conquer the land. Best of all, after Moses died, God chose Joshua to be the brave captain who led the people into that land.

Prayer

Dear God, I don't ever want to be a coward. But sometimes I feel alone and am afraid. When this happens, help me to remember that you are always with me and will give me courage. In Jesus' name, amen.

Questions

1. Why did Moses send scouts into Canaan?
2. What two reports did the scouts bring back?

3. Why were the reports different?

4. Which report did the people believe?

5. What do you think of the saying, "The majority is always right"?

6. Can you be a leader for good causes if you always follow the crowd? How hard do you think it was for Joshua and Caleb to give their report when the other ten scouts were saying the opposite?

7. What are some of your fears? What do you do about them? How can God help you with them?

First Day in School

1 Samuel 1

I'm sure you know how happy your father and mother were the day you were born, and how they thanked God for you. But did you ever stop to think how much they wanted you and how many times they prayed for you, even before you were born?

Well, in the Bible there's a story about a father and mother — their names were Elkanah and Hannah — who did all this for their little son, Samuel, plus one thing more.

❧   ❧   ❧

Elkanah, Hannah, and three-year-old Samuel were very tired. They were on their way to the temple in Shiloh and had been traveling all day. As they reached the top of the next hill, Elkanah said, "Look, there in the valley is a grove of trees. Nearby there must be a spring. That's where we'll pitch our tent and spend the night."

Before long, they had finished their supper and were resting beside their campfire. "Samuel," said Hannah to her little son, "your father and I are so proud that you can grow up in God's house in Shiloh. We know you'll be so much help to Eli, the priest, in his work in the temple."

"But, Mother, what can I do?" asked Samuel.

"Many things, my son. You can open the doors each morning and sweep the floors. You can water the flowers and help take care of the garden. At night you can light the lamps. When you're a little older, you can help the priest with the worship services. Eli will be your teacher. You will learn many things about God and his world and what God expects you to be."

"Mother, tell me again about the time you asked God for a son," said Samuel.

"Well, your father and I often asked God for a child. We had been married for several years, but still we had no children. More than anything else in the world we wanted a baby. So once year when we were at the temple to offer our sacrifices, I went into the temple to pray. I promised God that if he would send me a son, later I would bring him here so he could grow up under the care of the priest and be trained to do God's work. You are the gift God sent in answer to my prayer."

"That's why we named you Samuel," explained Elkanah. "Your name means 'asked of God.'"

"You'll like Eli," said Hannah. "I'll never forget how kind he was to me that day when I prayed in the temple. As I was leaving, he put his hand on my head and said, 'Go in peace, and may God answer your prayer.' And now, Samuel, it's time for us to go to sleep."

When the family arrived in Shiloh the next day, they took the bull they had brought along and sacrificed it to the Lord, as they did every year. Then they went to see Eli. "This is our son Samuel," said Elkanah after Eli had greeted them.

"What a fine boy!" Eli exclaimed. "How I wish I could find someone like him to live with me and help me with my duties here!"

"That's the reason we've come," said Hannah. "When I prayed for a son I promised God that, if he answered my prayer, I would bring my son here to be his servant in the temple."

Eli was very pleased. "I'll take care of you as if you were my own son," Eli said to Samuel. "Perhaps you'll grow up to be a prophet."

"What's a prophet?" Samuel asked.

"A man who speaks to the people for God," answered Eli, "a man who helps them to know God and to understand what God wants them to do."

"I think I'd like to be a prophet when I grow up," said Samuel.

"Before Elkanah and I go back home," Hannah said to Eli, "may we go inside the temple and show Samuel the place where I asked God to send us a son?"

"Of course," said Eli. He turned to lead the way. At the door he stopped. "Samuel," he said, "you are my helper now, so you may open the door." That pleased Samuel very much. When they came to the place where Hannah had prayed for a son, Eli asked them all to kneel. Then he prayed for God to bless all of them, especially Samuel in his new home and his new work. Do you understand why from then on that was a very special place in the temple for Samuel, and why he so often knelt there to pray during the years that followed?

After Hannah and Elkanah had left for home, Eli stooped down and put his arm around Samuel and said, "You have such a wonderful father and mother! I'm sure you're going to be just the boy I need and that you'll become the prophet God needs."

So Samuel lived in Shiloh with his friend and teacher, Eli the priest, and helped him every day with his duties in the temple. As they worked together week after week, Samuel learned not only about God but also about the needs of the people as they came to worship.

This was God's way of preparing him to become the great and good prophet he later did become — a prophet so loved and honored that two of the books in our Bible are named for him!

Prayer

Dear God, I thank you for parents who wanted and prayed for me before I was born, and for the way I have been loved and cared for ever since. I thank you, too, for teachers who have helped me to learn more about you and your world so I can become the person you want me to be. Give me the joy of always doing my best. In Jesus' name, amen.

Questions

1. Why did Elkanah and Hannah bring Samuel to Eli?
2. What did Samuel learn from Eli?
3. What do you think Samuel did to help Eli?
4. What are some of the things you can do to help your church?
5. Ask your father or mother to tell you what they said to God when you were born and to explain their hopes for you.
6. What can you do to help make their hopes come true?
7. Discuss some of the ways that people today give their time to God.

Surprise Package

1 Samuel 2:12-26; 3

Where do you go to school? Most likely you go to a school not far from where you live, so you're at home every night. But suppose for some reason your parents enrolled you in a boarding school several hundred miles away. Suppose, too, that they were able to come to visit you only once a year. What could they do and what could you do to keep your love alive and warm?

Samuel grew up in the temple. His mother, Hannah, had promised God that if he would give her a son, she would give her son back to him — and that's exactly what happened. Samuel's parents visited him every year when they traveled to Shiloh to offer sacrifices to God. They were proud of the way he served as the helper of Eli the priest, and he loved them very much.

❧   ❧   ❧

It had been a busy day for Samuel. Hundreds of people had come to

Shiloh to offer their sacrifices at the temple. All day long Samuel had helped Eli greet them and prepare their sacrifices.

Now that night had come, he was tired but happy — happy because among those who had come to Shiloh were his father and mother, Elkanah and Hannah. At last he could sit down and talk with them.

"Son," said Elkanah, "we can see that you're a great help to Eli."

"He told us this morning that he couldn't get along without you," Hannah added. "We're proud of you, Samuel."

"Eli is very kind to me," Samuel replied. "I try to help him all I can."

Then Hannah gave Samuel a small package. "It's a present from us," she said.

"Oh, Mother!" Samuel exclaimed as he opened it. It was a little brown woolen coat! His mother had made it herself — in those days there were no clothing factories or department stores.

"Something to keep you warm," explained Hannah as she helped him put it on.

"It fits just right!" exclaimed Samuel, very excited.

"It will remind you of how much we love you," Hannah said.

"I already knew that — and I love you, too," Samuel replied, as he threw his arms around his parents and kissed them.

"Listen, Samuel," Hannah said. "I'm going to make you a promise. Since you're away from home helping Eli and serving God in the temple, I'm going to bring you a new coat every year."

And Hannah kept her promise. She brought Samuel a new coat every year when she and Elkanah came to Shiloh to worship in the temple. Each time the three of them would sit and have a nice long visit. Samuel would tell his parents what he and Eli had been doing, and his parents would tell him about what was happening back home.

Since they had had several more children since Samuel had been born — three sons and two daughters — they would bring them along so Samuel could meet his brothers and sisters.

On one of these visits, they began to discuss Eli. "He seemed very sad when we saw him this morning," Elkanah said. "Do you think he's worried about something?"

"Yes, I know he is," answered Samuel. "He's worried about his two sons, Hophni and Phinehas. They steal from the people who come to the temple and do many other things they shouldn't do. A few nights ago, God told me about them."

"Tell us about it," said Hannah.

"I had just gone to bed,"

Samuel began, "when I heard someone calling my name. I thought it was Eli, so I jumped up and ran to him. But he said he hadn't called me. Two more times I heard the voice, and two more times I went to Eli. Each time he said he hadn't called me. The third time he said, 'Samuel, perhaps God is calling you. If he calls again, say that you are his servant, and that you are listening.'

"When I had gone back to bed again, I heard the voice calling. I did what Eli had told me to do — I said, 'Speak, Lord, for I am your servant, and I am listening.' Then God told me that Eli's two sons were very wicked and that he would never allow them to take their father's place as priests in the temple."

"Does Eli know about this?" Elkanah asked.

"Yes," said Samuel. "The next morning he asked me about it, so I told him."

"No wonder he's sad," Elkanah remarked. "What a heavy burden — to have two sons like that."

"I'm so glad that we don't have to worry about you, Samuel," Hannah said, as she put her arms around him and gave him a hug.

"Perhaps it will be God's plan for you to take Eli's place someday," said Elkanah. "If so, I know you won't fail him."

Elkanah was right. Samuel did grow up to be a great prophet, and he did eventually take Eli's place as priest. He learned many lessons while he was growing up with Eli. He learned not to be like Eli's sons. And he learned to love and honor his parents, who also loved him very much. Who can say how much their yearly visits and their constant love shaped the man Samuel became? And who can say how much the loving care of our parents helps us to become the men and women God wants us to be?

Prayer

Dear God, thank you for parents, teachers, and friends who show their love for me by being kind. Thank you for the many ways they help and encourage me. Help me to show how grateful I am by being kind to them and to all who need help that I can give. In Jesus' name, amen.

Questions

1. Why was Eli worried?
2. What did God tell Samuel when he called to him? If you had been Samuel, how would you have felt about God's message to you?
3. Why did "the little coat" mean so much to Samuel?
4. What were some of the ways Samuel showed his gratitude for his parents' love?
5. List some of the gifts your mother and father have given you.
6. In what ways can you show them how grateful you are?
7. List some of God's gifts to you.
8. How can you show God how grateful you are?

The Reluctant King

1 Samuel 8–10

The people of the United States have what is called a presidential election every four years. At that time the people go to places called polls and vote. In this way they decide who will be the next president of the United States.

But for several months before the election, the individuals who want to be president — they're called candidates — travel around the country making speeches. It's clear from these speeches that all of the candidates want to be elected. But they often sound very proud and arrogant.

What do you suppose would happen if one of them said instead that he didn't feel worthy of the honor? Would that be a sign that he would make a good president?

❧   ❧   ❧

Many years ago the people of Israel were trying to decide whether or not to have a king. Almost everyone was in favor of the idea, but Samuel was against it.

Samuel was Israel's prophet, and usually they looked to him for guidance. He warned them how much it would cost to support a king and his court, but the people still wanted one. He also pointed out that God was their king, but they wanted a human king.

"We need someone to fight our battles and to defend us against our enemies," they said. "Besides, other nations have kings, and we want to be like them."

So Samuel gave in and promised that, with God's help, he would find them one. Then he asked God to help him find the right man. "Tomorrow I will send him to you," God answered.

Sure enough, the next afternoon Samuel saw a young man whom he had never seen before coming with his servant up the hill toward his house. Samuel noticed that he was very tall and handsome. Then a voice said, "This is the man I have chosen, the one who will be the king of my people."

The man's name was Saul, and for three days he and his servant had walked here and there over the land searching for some donkeys that had strayed away from his father's farm. They had asked all the people they met along the way if they had seen any stray donkeys, but no one had. So on this, the afternoon of the third day, Saul said to his servant, "I don't like to give up, but by now my father will be worrying about us. Maybe we should go back home."

But the servant said, "I have heard that nearby, in the town of Ramah, lives a prophet who is a wise man of God. Perhaps he can help us find the donkeys."

"A good idea," Saul replied.

So they took the road to Ramah. When they arrived in the city, the first person they met was Samuel, but of course they didn't know who he was.

"Pardon me, sir," said Saul. "Can you tell us where the prophet lives?"

"I am the prophet," Samuel answered, "and over there is my house.

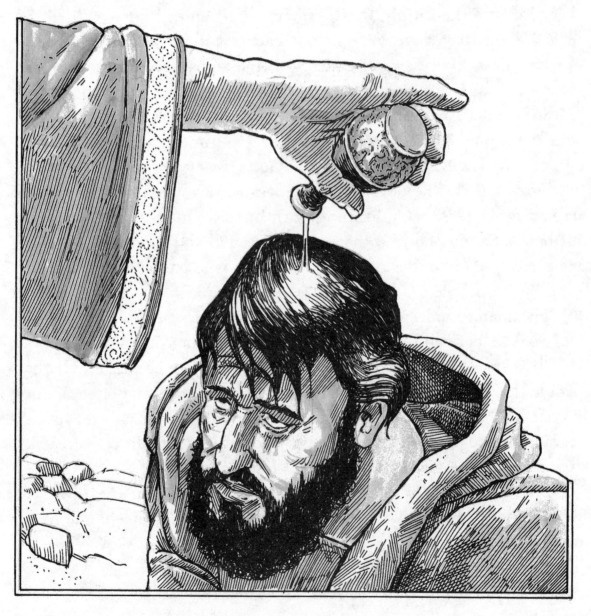

Come with me up this hill. There's a feast in the city today, and you will be my guests. Don't worry about the donkeys that were lost — they're already back at your father's home. Tomorrow I will tell you whatever you want to know, and then you can leave. But today, come to the feast. You are what all of Israel wants."

Saul couldn't believe it! How did Samuel know about the donkeys before he and his servant had even asked about them? And why would all of Israel be interested in *him?* "But I'm from the tribe of Benjamin," he said to Samuel, "the smallest of all the twelve tribes of Israel. And my family is one of the least known in our tribe! Why do you say the things you do?" But Samuel didn't answer. He just led the way to the feast.

So Saul went to dinner with Samuel. There, to his great surprise, he was given the chief seat and was served first — as if the dinner had been prepared in his honor! And he spent the night in Samuel's house.

The next morning, when Saul and his servant were ready to leave, Samuel walked with them a little way. When they came to the edge of the city, Samuel asked Saul to send his servant on ahead. Then from his coat he took a small bottle of oil and poured it on Saul's head, saying as he did, "God has anointed you to be the king and captain of his people! He will be with you to help you."

Several days later, Samuel called the people together in the city of Mizpah, where he promised to introduce them to their new king.

When the day arrived, all the tribes of Israel were assembled, ready to hear what Samuel had to say. Samuel said, "I promised to find a man to be your king. Then I asked God to lead me to the right man, and he has answered my prayer. The one whom he has chosen is from the tribe of Benjamin. His father's name is Kish, and his name is Saul. I ask him to come now and stand beside me so that all of you may see and welcome him."

Of course, people were looking all around, eager for a glimpse of the new king. But would you believe it? Saul didn't come forward! Once again that feeling of humility and unworthiness had come over him, and he had slipped away to hide. No one could find him!

Then God spoke to Samuel: "Have someone look in the tent where the baggage is."

Sure enough, there he was! When he was brought out, the people saw that he stood head and shoulders above everyone else. From all sides, expressions of praise and admiration were heard:

"How tall he is!" said one.

"And strong!" a second said.

"And handsome!" a third exclaimed.

"Just the right man!" a fourth shouted.

When at last Saul was standing by Samuel, Samuel laid his hand on Saul's shoulder and said, "This is the man God has chosen to be your king. See for yourselves — there is no one else like him among you!"

The people agreed as they raised their hands high in the air and shouted at the top of their voices: "Long live the king! Long live the king!"

This is how Saul, the son of Kish, became the first king of the nation of Israel. What a great honor! But also, what a great responsibility!

Prayer

Dear God, if I am ever chosen for something special, may it make me feel humble and grateful but not proud. Then may I do my best not to fail, and may I trust you to help me. And thank you for all the times you have already helped me. In Jesus' name, amen.

Questions

1. Why did the people of Israel ask for a king? When is it hardest for you to do things God's way and not be "like everyone else"?
2. What did Samuel say before he gave in to the people?
3. What circumstances did God arrange so that Saul and Samuel could meet?
4. Why did Saul hesitate to accept the honor of becoming king?
5. Make a list of the good qualities you find in Saul as you think back upon this story.
6. Why are proud people sometimes unpopular?
7. Why should you be humble and not proud about the gifts God has given you?
8. What can you do to keep from being too proud?

When the Last Was First

1 Samuel 16:1-13; Acts 13:22

I f you were left out of something you very much wanted to be a part of, and if you were left out because you were too young or too little, how would you feel? Well, if you were a good sport about it and didn't grumble or complain, and then later you realized that it all turned out for the best, that would make it okay, wouldn't it?

That's just what happened to a shepherd boy named David.

🎋   🎋   🎋

David loved all seven of his brothers, but sometimes he wished he were not the youngest. Often when his brothers were starting to play a game or planning to go somewhere, one of them would say, "You're too little, David," and he would be left out. Even when he was older, whenever "someone" had to stay behind, he was always the one.

On one particular morning, David wanted more than anything else in the world to be able to go to Bethlehem. Everybody in and around the town was excited because the prophet Samuel was coming to offer a special sacrifice to God, and it was rumored that at noon he would announce who would be the next king of Israel. But that morning David's father, Jesse, said, "David, someone has to take care of the sheep. I want you to do that today while we go to the sacrifice."

David did as he was told — he didn't argue with his father. But all that morning, while the sheep were grazing in the valley, he was sitting under a tree playing his harp, wondering what was going on in Bethlehem and wishing he could be there.

He had just finished his lunch when he saw two of his brothers, Abinadab and Shammah, running over the hill toward him. Abinadab was shouting, "David, David, come quick!"

"I'll stay and watch the sheep," said Shammah. "You go with Abinadab."

As they hurried along, Abinadab told David what had happened back in Bethlehem.

"Soon after the prophet Samuel arrived," he said, "he came over to our father and said, 'Jesse, God has revealed to me that one of your sons is to be the next king of Israel. I want you to bring them to me, one by one.'

"Eliab came first. We all thought he would be the one, because he's the oldest, the tallest, and very handsome. But the prophet said, 'God has not chosen him.' Then he added, 'People look at the outside of a man, but God looks at the heart.'

"I was next, then Shammah, then our four other brothers, but in each case Samuel said, 'This is not the one.'

"At last he turned to our father and said, 'Are these all your sons?' Then Father told him about you, and the prophet said, 'Send for him. We won't offer the sacrifice until he comes.'"

At last Abinadab and David arrived, red-faced and panting, and made their way through the crowd to the place where Samuel and Jesse were standing beside the altar.

"This is my youngest son. His name is David," Jesse said to Samuel.

"David," said Samuel, "before I came to Bethlehem, God revealed to me that one of your father's sons would be the next king of Israel, but I didn't know which one. All seven of your brothers have come before me. In each case, God said, 'This is not the one.' But when you came, God said, 'Rise and anoint him, for he is the one.' God has chosen you; one day you will be king of Israel."

Then David dropped to his knees, and Samuel poured oil upon his head, saying, "May the Lord bless you and make you a good king." After that, it didn't bother David anymore that he was the youngest in his

family. Later he did become a noble king, as Samuel had prayed he would. He was a ruler known far and wide as "a man after God's own heart."

Prayer

Dear God, no matter how young I am, I believe you have a noble plan for my life. Help me to be a good student at school and a cheerful helper at home so I will be prepared to fulfill your will with my life. In Jesus' name, amen.

Questions

1. Why did Samuel come to Bethlehem?
2. Why was one of Jesse's older sons not chosen to be the next king?
3. What have you learned from this story about judging people by appearance?
4. Why wasn't David in the city when Samuel came to Bethlehem? How did David feel about that?
5. Can you think of a time when you were disappointed about something, but later it turned out for the best? What happened?
6. What should that teach you about faith? About patience?
7. The Bible says that David was a "man after God's own heart" (see Acts 13:22). Do you think it could be said that you are a person "after God's own heart"?
8. How do you believe God wants to use you in his work? What should you be doing now to be prepared?

Superboy

1 Samuel 17

Do you like stories about Batman, Tarzan, and Superman? Well, did you ever stop to think that you don't have to have superhuman powers to be "super"? The Bible tells us about a simple shepherd boy who proved he really was "super."

One evening in Bethlehem, a man named Jesse called his son to his side. "David," he said, "tomorrow I want you to take a basket of food to your three brothers and find out how they are and how the battle is going."

At this time King Saul was leading Israel's army in a battle with the Philistines, a warlike people who lived along the seashore of Palestine. These people often attacked the farms and villages of those Israelites who lived in the hills, and Saul wanted to stop these raids.

David's three oldest brothers had joined Saul's army, and it was to them that David was being sent by his father.

David started out early the next morning, went to the place where Saul's army was camped, and soon found his brothers. They were glad to have the food David had brought and also to hear the news from home.

Suddenly a great shout was heard from the camp of the Philistines, which was across the valley on the opposite hill. David and his brothers could see the leader of the Philistines, a big giant named Goliath. He was walking back and forth in front of the Philistine camp, waving his spear high in the air and shouting across the valley, "Choose your strongest man and let him come over and fight with me. If he can kill me, then my people will become your slaves. But if I kill him, then your people will become our slaves. I dare any man to come over and fight me."

But all the men in Saul's army were afraid — not one accepted the dare. David thought this was a disgrace. So he said to some of the soldiers, "I'll go fight him."

When Eliab, David's oldest brother, heard about this, he said, "Come on! You don't know anything about fighting! Go watch the sheep! Who do you think you are, anyway?"

When Saul heard about David's courage, he sent for him. When he saw David was younger than all his soldiers, he said, "You're too young to fight, and you've never been in a battle. The giant has been a man of war for years."

"I'm not afraid of him," David replied. "For a long time I tended my father's sheep, and whenever a bear or a lion tried to steal one of the lambs from the flock, I killed him. Killing this giant will be just like killing one of these lions or bears. And God will help me."

When Saul saw that David was determined, he gave David his bronze helmet and his armor. But these things were too big and too heavy for David — they swallowed him up! So he took them off and started down the hill with just his shepherd's tunic on, his shepherd's staff in one hand and his sling in the other.

Do you wonder why he decided to fight the giant? I think he did that because he knew that God had chosen him to be the next king of Israel. Samuel the prophet had already anointed him in Bethlehem, and David felt that he must be brave and strong and not allow Goliath to get away with his dare.

That sling David carried at his side was one he had made with his own hands. He had practiced and practiced with it until he could hit the target almost every time.

When David reached the valley, he stopped at the shallow stream there and bent down to get some of the small stones that covered the bottom of the stream. His father had taught him what kind of stones were best for slings, so he was very careful about the ones he selected. He found five that were smooth and round, about the size of an egg. These he placed in a little bag tied to his waist. Then he started up the hill toward the giant. Saul and his army were watching in spellbound silence from the hill behind him.

When David got near Goliath, he noticed that Goliath's entire body was covered with armor, and that he was armed with a sword and a spear and a javelin. When he saw David, he laughed out loud and made fun of him: "Boy, how did you ever get away from your mother? You come after me with a stick and a handful of rocks — do you think I'm a dog? Come after me, and I'll feed you to the birds and wild animals!"

David answered back, "You come against me with a sword and a spear and a javelin, but I come against you in the name of the Lord

God of Israel, whom you have defied. He's on our side,
and he will give me the victory over you so that all these
people may know that he is the true God. I'm not afraid
of you, because God is with us!"

David slipped one of the stones into his sling and
began whirling it around and around. As Goliath came closer,
David noticed that there was a spot right between his eyes that wasn't
covered by his helmet. So he aimed straight for that spot as Goliath
rushed at him.

Swift and straight the stone sped to its mark, hitting the giant
right between the eyes. That stopped him cold! He stood still for a
second, then fell forward on his face.

At that moment a loud shout came up from behind David as the army of Israel rushed forward toward the Philistine camp. The Philistines, seeing that their leader had fallen, started running as fast as they could in the opposite direction, with the Israelite soldiers right behind them.

So, because of the courage and skill of David, the army of Israel won a great victory over the Philistines. For many weeks afterward, people on all sides kept talking about David and singing his praises. But in all Israel no one could have been more pleased than the prophet Samuel, for he knew that the day David would become a brave and noble king could not be far away.

Prayer

Dear God, help me to be as brave in meeting my temptations as David was in meeting Goliath. May I remember that I never have to fight alone, but that you are always ready to help me just as you helped David. Teach me, too, that no temptation is too strong if I use my willpower and your help. In Jesus' name, amen.

Questions

1. Why did David go to the camp of Saul's army?
2. What made Saul's soldiers so afraid?
3. Why did King Saul send for David?

4. What was the secret of David's skill with a sling?

5. What qualities do you see in David that make him worthy to be called "super"?

6. What was the secret of David's courage? How can you develop that kind of courage?

7. What are some of the enemies you must conquer to be a superboy or a supergirl?

The Best of Friends

1 Samuel 18–20

One of the most important things in life is friendship. Friendship is often based on what two people have in common and the good times they have together. But it is also based on trust, loyalty, and unselfishness. The Bible tells us about two young men who not only said they were the best of friends but *showed* they were the best of friends in their behavior toward each other.

When David came back to the camp after his victory over the giant Goliath, King Saul, who had watched the battle, asked that David be brought to his tent so he could reward him for his brave deed.

There Saul introduced him to another young man standing beside him: "This is my son, Jonathan. You and he should become good friends because, to reward you for what you've done, I'm going to take you home with us. Your brothers who are in my army may return to Bethlehem and tell your father."

"Whatever the king says, I will do," David replied.

Then Jonathan shook hands with David and said, "David, I'm glad to be your friend!" And Jonathan really meant it, because the Bible tells us, "From that time, his soul was knit to the soul of David, and he loved him as his own soul" — which means that he really loved David as much as he loved himself.

In a way, it was strange that Jonathan and David should become such close friends because, you see, they were *rivals*. Both of them were in line to become the next king of Israel. Jonathan was in line because he was the son of Saul, Israel's first king. And David was in line because the prophet Samuel had anointed him before a great crowd in Bethlehem and had declared that he was God's choice to be the next king. Of course, Saul hadn't heard about this when he took David home with him.

For a while Saul was good to David. He made him an officer in his army, and God made everything David did go well. But as the people kept on praising David, Saul began to be jealous of his popularity. One day, as David was playing his harp in the palace (he was a fine musician as well as a brave soldier), Saul, in a fit of anger, threw his spear at him, trying to kill him. But David escaped.

Saul was afraid of David, so he tried to get rid of him. First Saul sent David into battle as captain over a thousand men. He did this because he hoped David would be killed in battle. When that didn't work, he promised that David could marry one of his daughters if David first killed a hundred Philistines. The truth was that Saul hoped David would be killed in the fighting. But David was successful again.

In fact, he killed two hundred Philistines, so Saul had no choice but to let David marry his daughter.

Now Saul was desperate, so desperate that he told his servants and Jonathan to kill David. At this point Jonathan stepped in to help David. He warned David about Saul, then went to talk to his father.

"Remember how David helped you by killing Goliath?" Jonathan reminded him. "He has done nothing against you. Why do you want to kill him?" Saul listened to Jonathan, and he allowed David to be with him again.

Again war broke out, and again David went to serve in the army. He was so successful that Saul's jealousy returned. A second time he threw his spear at David while he was playing his harp. Again David escaped, and again Saul pursued him. When Saul couldn't kill him at the palace, he sent messengers to David's house to try to kill him there. In the end David fled the city and stayed with Samuel for awhile.

Later he returned to see Jonathan and talk with him. "Why does your father try to kill me, Jonathan? What have I done wrong?"

"You haven't done anything wrong," Jonathan assured him. "I don't think my father really wants to kill you. He tells me everything, and he hasn't said anything about killing you."

But David answered, "Your father knows that you and I are friends. He doesn't want to hurt you by letting you know, but I'm sure he wants to kill me."

Jonathan was concerned when he heard this. "Whatever you want me to do, I'll do it," he said.

"You're a true and wonderful friend, Jonathan," said David gratefully. "I thank God for you! Tomorrow I'm supposed to have dinner with your father, but I'm not going to show up. When he asks why I'm not there, speak kindly about me. If he doesn't get angry, then we'll know I'm safe. But if he loses his temper, then we'll know he wants to harm me."

"I'll talk to him," Jonathan said. "I know God has chosen you to be the next king, and I'm sure you'll be a good king."

Then the two men made a covenant together and promised each

other that no matter what happened, they would always be true friends. After that, at Jonathan's suggestion, David hid in a large field.

Two days later, when David still hadn't shown up at the palace for meals, Saul asked where he was. Jonathan gave a reasonable answer, but Saul became very angry. He called Jonathan an ugly name and shouted, "That's enough, Jonathan! Can't you see it will cost you your crown if you keep on being David's friend? As long as he's alive, you will never be king. That's why he must die! Now bring him to me."

"Father," Jonathan answered, "you shouldn't be angry with David — he's loyal to you and has never done anything against you." At that, Saul's anger exploded, and he threw his spear at Jonathan! Now Jonathan knew that his father intended to kill David, and now *he* became very angry. He left the table without eating and later went out to the field where David was hiding. Using a special signal, Jonathan indicated to David that he was in danger. The news was so sad that both of the men cried, then renewed their promise to each other that they would always be true friends.

"Jonathan," David said, "you mean so much to me that I can't express my feelings in words. But this I promise: if God keeps me alive and I do become king, you will be next to me in my kingdom!"

David really meant that promise. Later he did become king, but before that time, sad to say, Jonathan was killed while fighting bravely in a battle against the Philistines. But long after Jonathan was dead, David still remembered him and loved him.

Prayer

Dear God, help me to remember that the way to have friends is to be friendly. Then make me as kind and unselfish toward my friends as Jonathan was to David. And thank you, dear God, for the kind of friend you are to me. In Jesus' name, amen.

Questions

1. Why did Saul take David home with him?
2. Why did he later hate David?
3. What did David do when Saul tried to kill him?
4. What promise did David and Jonathan make to each other?
5. Could you be a friend to someone who got something you wanted? How can you be more like Jonathan, who loved David even though he knew that David would become king instead of him?
6. Do you get angry or jealous easily? What can you do about it?
7. Thinking of David and Jonathan, how would you describe a true friend?

Whose Baby?

1 Kings 3:3-28

Perhaps you know the Greek fable about King Midas.

One day Bacchus, one of the Greek gods, wanted to reward King Midas for a good deed. He said to him, "Whatever you wish for, you may have."

Now, as a child, King Midas had been very poor, so he said to Bacchus, "I want to be rich, so my wish is that everything I touch may turn to gold."

Bacchus knew King Midas had made a very foolish choice, but he gave him what he asked for just the same.

At first, King Midas was thrilled! He picked up a stick, a stone, an apple — and each turned to gold in his hand! But soon he began to realize that his wish had a dark side. Arriving home, he ordered his servants to prepare a big banquet. But when he sat down to enjoy the feast, the bread he picked up turned to gold and broke his teeth when he tried to bite it. The wine in his glass became molten gold when he tried to drink it. He even turned his daughter to gold when he touched her.

Desperate, he begged Bacchus to deliver him from the curse which he had thought would be a blessing. He was told to go and bathe in the river. By doing that, he finally washed away his sin of greed and learned that there are other things in life more important than money.

This story is about a real king who was given a choice very much like the one that was offered to King Midas. But his wish was much wiser than the wish made by King Midas.

❧   ❧   ❧

After David died, his son, Solomon, became the next king of Israel. At the beginning of his reign, he was a very good king.

One night soon after he became king, God came to him in a dream and said, "What would you like me to give you?"

Solomon's answer was a prayer. "O Lord," he said, "my father, David, was a wise and good king. Compared with him, I feel like a little child. But you have made me king in his place, and your people have become a great nation.

"I'm not wise enough to rule over them. So give me, I pray, a wise and understanding heart so that I may know the difference between right and wrong and be able to rule with justice and fairness to all."

God was very pleased by this prayer. It showed that Solomon was thinking more of his duty to his people than of his own fame or happiness. And God said: "You might have asked for wealth, or for a long life, or for success in war, but instead you have asked for wisdom. So I will give you what you have asked for." And God kept his promise and gave Solomon a wise and understanding mind.

One of the many cases that came before Solomon for judgment was an argument between two women.

One of the women said, "Your Majesty, this woman and I live in the same house. That baby in her arms is mine. Her own baby died in the night, and while I was asleep, she stole my baby from my side and put her dead baby in my bed. I didn't know what she had done until I woke up this morning and found her dead baby beside me."

"No, no!" said the other woman. "The living baby is mine. The dead baby is hers."

"She's telling a lie!" exclaimed the first woman. "The dead baby belongs to her. She stole my baby while I slept. Make her give it back!"

Solomon knew, of course, that one of the women was telling a lie. He said to himself, "The woman that loves the living baby the most is the real mother. To find out which one she is, I will put them both to a test."

"Bring me the baby," he said to the woman who had the child. Then Solomon handed the baby to a soldier standing by his throne, and called to another soldier to bring him a sword. The two women stepped back, shocked at what the king was about to do.

"Now," said Solomon. "Both of you claim the living baby is yours. So I'll divide it, and then each of you can have half."

Of course, Solomon had no idea of hurting the baby. He was only "play-acting" or pretending to see what the two women would do.

He had hardly finished speaking when one of them rushed forward and threw herself at his feet. "No, no, Your Majesty! Don't harm the baby. Give it to the other woman and let her keep it. But don't touch it with your sword!"

But the other woman said, "Divide the baby. Then it will be neither mine nor hers."

"This is the baby's mother," said Solomon, pointing to the woman who spoke first. "She's the one who really loves it. Give the baby to her."

All who heard this story were amazed by Solomon's wisdom, and he was honored far and wide as one of the wisest kings that ever lived.

Prayer

Dear God, I pray that you will make me more like Solomon, that you will give me the wisdom to know right from wrong. I also pray that when I know what is right, I will always stand up for it, and stand against what is wrong. In Jesus' name, amen.

Questions

1. How did Solomon feel when he compared himself with his father, David?
2. What could Solomon have asked for other than wisdom?
3. Why was his prayer a good one?
4. What were the two mothers arguing about?
5. How did Solomon show his wisdom?
6. If God made you the same offer he made to Solomon, what would you ask for?
7. What do you think it means to be wise? (See Job 28:28 and Matthew 7:24-25.)
8. What is the difference between knowledge and wisdom?
9. Do you know someone who has wisdom?

Good Advice and Bad

1 Kings 12:1-24; 14:21-31

If you had an important decision to make, or for some other reason
you needed advice, to whom would you turn? To your mother or
father? To one of your teachers? To your minister? To a group of your
friends?

Well, regardless of where you would go, you can be sure of one
thing: if someone advises you to be kind, that's always good advice,
and if someone advises you to be selfish, that's always bad advice.

This story is about a king who found that out the hard way!

※   ※   ※

For Rehoboam it was the most important day of his life, the day he
was to be crowned king of Israel, and he was very excited. Under the
reign of his father, Solomon, the nation had become richer and more
powerful than it had ever been before, and the throne was about to

become his. No wonder his spirits were high as he put on his royal robe in preparation for the ceremony that would make him king.

But a surprise was in store for him that was anything but pleasant. It was something like a labor union showing up and threatening to strike unless the president of the company met their demands. Only in this case the discontented people made their demands of the new king. The spokesman for the "union" was a courageous man by the name of Jeroboam. And this is what he said to Rehoboam, speaking for the people he represented:

"Your father, Solomon, was known far and wide for his wisdom and for his building achievements. You remember that he spent seven years building the temple in Jerusalem and thirteen more building his palace. But those were twenty years of backbreaking labor for many of us. Thirty thousand of us were drafted to go to the land of Lebanon, over a hundred miles north of Jerusalem, to cut the lumber needed and bring it down to Jerusalem. As you know, we worked in shifts — ten thousand of us were sent to work for a month in the forest of Lebanon, then sent back home for two months before being sent back to Lebanon for another month — and this went on for several years. Others of us were forced to work in rock quarries to provide the stones needed to help build the many new cities your father built and fortified.

"In short," Jeroboam concluded, "your father, Solomon, made our burdens heavy, and we ask you now to make them lighter. If you do this, you can count on us to support and serve you as long as you live."

Of course, Rehoboam hadn't expected anything like this on the day of his crowning, and he didn't know what to say. So he pleaded for time. "Give me three days to think over what you've told me," he said. "Come back after that, and I'll tell you what I will do."

That night — his first night as king — Rehoboam couldn't sleep because he was thinking about his new problem. This business of being king was turning out to be anything but a bed of roses. He decided he needed some advice — and soon!

So the next morning he called together a group of older men, men who had been counselors to his father and who were well acquainted with the affairs of the kingdom.

"What answer do you advise me to give to these people?" he asked.

After conferring together they answered, "In many ways your father was a great king, but it is true that he demanded too much of his people and that their burdens were heavy. Therefore, we advise you to speak kindly to them and to make their burdens lighter. Think of yourself as their servant rather than their master, and then they will love you and be loyal to you as long as you live. Your father was a king known all over the world for his wisdom. Now this is your opportunity to be a king known all over the world for your kindness."

How wise Rehoboam would have been if he had followed that advice! But, sad to say, he rejected it. The next day he asked a different group for their advice. They were younger men whom Rehoboam had grown up with, men who might be called his "buddies" or "pals." And they weren't only young — they were selfish and ambitious.

"Don't even think of giving in to those complainers," they said. "If you do, they'll be back with new demands before you know it. Let them see from the beginning that you're a king with authority and that you can't be pushed around. Be a king, not a puppet."

One of these men thought he was being funny when he said, "Tell them your little finger is stronger than your father's thigh, and while he used whips to keep them in line, you'll use scorpions!" With that, they all laughed — even Rehoboam joined in.

But it wasn't funny to Jeroboam and the people when they came back the following day to hear these words from Rehoboam. As you may have guessed, they were not only deeply disappointed but very angry. Then and there they decided that Rehoboam would never be their king. Instead, they returned home and a few days later made Jeroboam their king — that is, ten of the twelve tribes of the nation did. That left Rehoboam only two tribes to rule over. In one day, by making one bad decision, he had lost 80 percent of his people.

From that time on, the Jewish people were divided into two kingdoms. The ten tribes in the northern part of the country were called Israel; their capital was the city of Samaria. The two tribes in the southern part of the country were called Judah; Jerusalem was their capital. Frequently during Rehoboam's seventeen-year reign and for many years afterward, wars broke out between the two nations. Also, since both kingdoms were divided and therefore weak, they became easy prey to armies from other nearby nations who frequently invaded their lands and destroyed them.

Finally, several hundred years after Rehoboam's reign, the powerful nations of Assyria and Babylonia captured and destroyed both Samaria and Jerusalem and took thousands of Jewish people back to their own land as slaves.

What a long, sad story it is — the things that happened to the Jewish people from the time of Rehoboam onward. And it all began when he, as the new young king, turned his back on good advice.

Think how different the story of those later years might have been if he had followed the good advice of the older men and had been a kind servant to his people instead of becoming a harsh and selfish king.

Prayer

Dear God, so often when I have to make a decision, I have to choose between good advice and bad. Give me the wisdom to choose the good advice and follow it to the end. In Jesus' name, amen.

Questions

1. Why was Rehoboam so excited at the beginning of this story?
2. What did Jeroboam and the people with him ask the new king to do?
3. To whom did Rehoboam turn for advice?
4. Whose advice did he follow?
5. What did Jeroboam and the people who followed him do after hearing the king's decision?
6. How much of his kingdom did Rehoboam lose as a result?
7. Describe what happened to the Jewish people in the years that followed and discuss what might have happened instead if Rehoboam had followed the wise advice of the older men.
8. Share with each other some of the good advice you have received. Tell who gave it to you and explain what you did about it.
9. What "good advice" do you think we find in the Bible?

Builders Together

1 Chronicles 22; 2 Chronicles 6

Have you ever walked into a beautiful church and looked at the high ceiling, the organ pipes, the lovely windows, and the pulpit or altar? Did anyone ever explain to you the meaning of the steeple, the cross, the crown, the candles, and other Christian symbols?

This story is about the first real temple the people of Israel had, built of stone and iron and wood — built because a father and son planned and worked together with perfect understanding to make their dream come true.

As you read the story, remember that your church too was once the dream of those who loved God and wanted to honor him by creating a beautiful place to worship him.

☙   ☙   ☙

The Bible doesn't tell us just when David, the king of Israel, and Solomon, his son, first talked together about building a temple in

Jerusalem, but it does tell us that it was a project that they planned together. So it's very possible that when Solomon was still a little boy, his favorite toy was a set of building blocks, given to him by his father, David, and that one day, as he played with his blocks, he called to David, who was sitting close by, and said, "Look, Father! See what I'm building."

"Yes, son, I see," said David, as he came closer. "What is it? Wait, let me guess. A fort?"

"No, not a fort."

"A house?"

"No, but you're getting close."

"A palace?"

"No, something finer than a palace."

"I give up. What could be finer than a palace?"

"A temple," answered Solomon, "a house for God."

"Yes, of course," said David. "You're right! God's house should be finer than a king's palace."

"If that's true, Father, then why isn't it?" Solomon asked.

"What do you mean?" asked David.

"The house we have for God here in Jerusalem isn't as fine as our palace," Solomon replied. "It's not even built of wood and stone. It's made of canvas — it's just a big tent. I think God's house should be the most beautiful house of all!"

"You are so right, my son," agreed David. "I've been thinking about that for a long time."

Several years later, Solomon was older and better able to understand his father's ideas about the temple. It was then that David told Solomon that he had been planning for a long time to build a temple in Jerusalem. He explained how he had been busy for several years, getting the materials ready — timber and stone and iron and bronze and gold and silver. Then he showed Solomon the drawings for the temple he had in mind.

"I like it," Solomon said, as they looked at the plans together. "I'm so glad you're going to build it."

"But I'm not going to build it," David answered. "God has revealed to me that you will be the next king after me, and that it is his plan for you to build the temple. So, my son, I want you to remember when you become king that you are to complete the work I have begun. The plans for the building will be yours, and all the materials I have collected will be yours. Also, I've told the chief men in the kingdom and my workmen to help you. I know you won't fail. Be strong and very brave, and never be discouraged. God himself will guide and help you. I pray that he will give you wisdom and strength to finish building his temple and also to keep his commands and be a good king."

Solomon never forgot those words of his father. When he became king some years later, one of the first things he did was to begin building the temple. He was careful to hire the most skillful and artistic workmen he could find and use only the very best of materials.

It took seven years to build the temple, and when it was finished it was so glorious that people came from far and near to see it and to worship God in it.

On the day it was dedicated, Solomon stood in front of the altar on a platform five feet high and, as the people bowed their heads, he offered this prayer:

"O God, how great you are! So great that all the sky around and above is not big enough for you to live in! How much smaller is this house we have built for your home! Still, may you listen to my prayer. Let your eyes be upon this place day and night, and when your people gather here to pray to you, hear their prayer and forgive their sins."

Then he added, "And blessed be the God of Israel, who put it into the heart of David my father to build a house to the glory of your name, and who helped me to complete my father's dream."

When Solomon had finished his noble prayer, all the people said "Amen."

Then the people probably sang a song written especially for the dedication, a song like this one:

How lovely is thy dwelling place,
O Lord of hosts! . . .
Blessed are those who dwell in thy house,
Ever singing thy praise! . . .
A day in thy courts is better
Than a thousand elsewhere.   [from Psalm 84]

With this song the service ended.

As you may know, for over five hundred years, until Jerusalem was destroyed by an army from Babylon, "Solomon's temple," as it was called, was the center of worship for the people of Israel.

While we know that God is everywhere and can be worshiped anywhere, we can be sure that he was greatly pleased that David and Solomon, as father and son, had worked together to create such a beautiful place for his people to come together to worship him.

Prayer

Dear God, just as David had dreams for Solomon, so my parents have dreams for me. Help me to cherish these dreams, and help me to realize them someday. And may I, like Solomon, love your house of worship, and whenever I go there, may I be thankful for all your many blessings. In Jesus' name, amen.

Questions

1. What did David tell Solomon about building the temple?
2. What was David's part in building the temple?
3. What was Solomon's part?
4. What are some things that you and your father or mother do as partners?
5. Tell what happened on the day the temple was dedicated.

6. Our churches today are like the temple. Why do you think it's important to have a special place to worship God?
7. Worship can also take place outside the church. In what other places and what other ways can we worship God?

Beauty Pageant

Esther 1–7

You have probably seen the Miss America beauty pageant on TV. Young women from every state in the nation come together to compete to see who will be crowned the most beautiful woman in the United States. You may think that this kind of contest is quite new, something not done in other times. But this story is about a beauty pageant held long ago in the land of Persia.

      ঽ   ঽ   ঽ

In the beginning, life wasn't easy for Esther. Her mother and father were among the Jews carried away to Babylon when Nebuchadnezzar captured Jerusalem about six hundred years before Jesus was born. (Remember, this happened to Daniel and his three friends, too.)

Esther was probably born in Babylon. When she was very young, both her parents died. She missed them very much, but it was her good fortune to be adopted by a noble cousin whose name was Mordecai.

[117]

He took her into his home and loved her and cared for her as if she were his own daughter.

By the time she became a young woman, she was very beautiful. Then one day her big opportunity came — to enter a nationwide beauty contest. The prize for the winner: a crown and a palace! You see, Ahasuerus, the king of Persia (the same country that was once called Babylon), had sent his queen away in a fit of anger and was looking for another one. Following the advice of his lords, he sent a notice to his 127 governors for each to choose a beautiful girl to send to his palace. From among these girls he himself would choose the new queen.

With Mordecai's approval, Esther entered the contest. But, since there was so much prejudice against Jews in Persia, Mordecai warned her

to tell no one about her race. Mordecai loved her so much and was so concerned about her that he walked back and forth in front of the palace every day during the contest, hoping to hear how she was getting along.

You can imagine how thrilled he was when he heard that she had won and that the king himself had placed the royal crown on her head! Esther had pleased the king, but not only because she was beautiful. He admired her because she had character.

Certainly Esther was pleased with all the advantages and luxuries she had as a queen. But it wasn't long before she learned that being a queen was sometimes as challenging as it was glamorous.

The king's prime minister, Haman, was a very proud man — so proud that when he rode through the streets of the city on his fine horse, he expected all the people to bow down to him, as if he were some kind of god! All the people did this, except one man — Mordecai!

This made Haman furious. And when he found out that Mordecai was a Jew, he got even angrier.

"I'll get even," he said to himself, "and more!" So he decided that Mordecai wasn't the only one who must die — *all* Jews in the whole kingdom of Persia must die!

The next morning he came to the king with a wicked lie and an evil plot.

"Your Majesty," he said, "all through your kingdom there is a race of people who are different from us and disloyal to you. They are against our government and do not keep our laws. I urge you to order them to be destroyed. I have with me a decree which will take care of everything, if Your Majesty will just sign it."

Haman didn't tell Ahasuerus that the people named in the decree were Jews. But when the king hesitated, he added, "And, to express my gratitude, I'm prepared to put into the king's treasury ten thousand pieces of silver."

How money talks! The king signed immediately! He didn't even look at the decree — his mind was on the ten thousand pieces of silver, a bribe equal to about eighteen million dollars in our money.

Mordecai was shocked when he heard about this decree, but what could he do? Nothing! But then he remembered Esther's position. Being the queen, she could do something!

So he sent her a message in which he told her about Haman's wicked plot and urged her to go to the king and plead with him to save the people.

But Esther was afraid to go.

"Everyone knows," she wrote back to Mordecai, "that there is a law in Persia that no one is allowed to go into the king's throne room without being called. If anyone goes in uninvited, he or she will be killed at once — unless the king holds out his golden scepter."

No wonder Esther was afraid! Mordecai understood, but he didn't want Esther to let her fear be an excuse for not doing her duty. So, he sent her a second message even more urgent than the first.

"You must go to the king anyway. If you don't, you won't escape either — you and your father's house will perish!" Then he added a question that really made Esther think:

"Who knows but what God made you queen for just such a time as this — so you would be able to save your people?"

In one way Esther probably thought of her crown as a prize which she had won and which she had every right to enjoy. But Mordecai's question reminded her that her crown was a gift from God to be used for his purposes.

Deep down in her heart, Esther knew Mordecai was right. And although she was still afraid, she sent back a brave answer.

"Call together all the Jews in the area and have them pray for me. My maids and I will pray, too. Then, after three days, I will go to the king, even though I know it's against the law. Even if I die, it will be all right, because I will have done my duty!"

So, after three days of prayer, Esther put on her royal robe and crown and, holding her head high, entered the throne room. The king's men were amazed when they saw her standing in the doorway, and they became suddenly silent, wondering what the king would do. To their great surprise, he rose and held out to her his golden scepter! In response, Esther came forward and touched the top of the scepter.

"Good morning, Queen Esther," said Ahasuerus. "What is your wish? Whatever it is, I will give it to you, even if you ask for half of my kingdom."

"If it please Your Majesty," Esther answered, "let the king and his prime minister come to my chambers this evening to a special dinner that I will prepare in the king's honor."

"We will be pleased to come," the king replied.

During the dinner, the king once again asked Esther what she wished for. But she delayed making her request, asking instead that the king and Haman return for dinner again the next night.

Haman was in high spirits because he was the only one of the king's ministers who had been invited to the queen's dinners. But as he left the palace, he passed Mordecai, who was one of the guards at the gate. Again Mordecai refused to bow down before him!

When he arrived home, he complained to his wife, Zeresh. "Here I am, one of the richest men in Persia, prime minister to the king, and the only one of his ministers invited to the queen's dinner tomorrow night! But what good is any of it as long as I see that Jew, Mordecai, standing in front of the palace and ignoring me?"

Then Zeresh said, "Cheer up! I'll tell you how to get rid of him! Have your servants build a gallows seventy-five feet high. Then, when you see the king tomorrow, ask him to order that Mordecai be hanged on it."

"Great idea!" said Haman. "I'll take care of it the first thing in the morning." What a cold-blooded couple!

Now it so happened that Ahasuerus couldn't sleep that night, so he got up to read. And in one of the books he read for the first time about how Mordecai some years back had heard about a plot to murder the king and had reported it in time to save the king's life.

The next morning, when Haman arrived at the palace, Ahasuerus was thinking about Mordecai and what should be done to reward him for his loyalty.

Haman was thinking about Mordecai too, and what lie he could tell the king so he would order Mordecai to be hanged.

Ahasuerus spoke first.

"Good morning, Mr. Prime Minister. I need your advice about a very important matter. What shall be done for the man to whom the king wishes to show special honor?"

Haman said to himself, "There's no one the king could wish to honor more than his prime minister — he must mean me!"

So he answered, "I have the perfect reward for the man to whom the king wishes to show special honor. Let him wear one of the king's royal robes and one of the king's crowns, and ride the king's own horse. Then let one of the king's most noble princes lead the horse around the center of the city, proclaiming, 'This is being done for the man whom the king is delighted to honor.'"

"Splendid!" exclaimed Ahasuerus. "You will be the noble prince to lead the horse. At the gate of the palace, ask for one of my guards named Mordecai. He once saved my life. He's the man to whom I wish to show special honor. Do everything for him you just described."

Inside Haman was saying, "Oh, no!" But he didn't dare refuse the king's request. So he had Mordecai dressed in the king's robe and put him on the king's horse. And he led the horse through the city square, proclaiming, "To this man the king is delighted to show special honor!"

That night, when Haman arrived for the queen's banquet, he was so depressed that he felt lower than a snake. But the worst was still to come!

Once he and the king were seated at the table, Ahasuerus said to Esther, "Now, what is your wish? Again I say, even if you ask for half of my kingdom, I will give it to you."

Then Esther told him about the cruel decree that called for the killing of the Jews throughout the land of Persia.

"They are my people," she added, "and it is *my wish* that no harm should come to them."

"Who is the man who would dare to do such a thing, and where is he?" Ahasuerus asked angrily.

"He is in this room, Your Majesty," Esther answered, "sitting right beside you! Your prime minister!"

And one of the king's attendants added, "And here's something else you don't know. He has built a gallows seventy-five feet high, and he plans to hang Mordecai, the man who saved your life!"

"You're right," said Ahasuerus. "Only last night I read how he once saved my life."

Then, turning to Haman, he said, "Now I see why you were so eager to offer me ten thousand pieces of silver to sign the decree! You didn't want me to know what was in it!

"Well, my clever prime minister, before I tell you that you're through, let me ask you just one more question: 'What shall be done to the man whom the king will be delighted to get rid of?'"

Haman's face went white with fear, and he was speechless.

"What, no answer to my question?" Ahasuerus continued after a pause. "But wait — you've already given me the answer!"

And the next morning who do you suppose was hanged on the seventy-five-foot-high gallows that Haman had built for Mordecai?

How grateful Mordecai must have been to Esther! And how proud of her courage!

At the risk of her own life she had saved his life and the lives of her people, and she had shown to all the world what a brave and unselfish queen she was! God had brought her to the throne for just such a time as this, and she had not failed him.

Prayer

Dear God, each day I have the opportunity to use the talents you have given to me. May I use them only for your glory and for the good of humanity. In Jesus' name, amen.

Questions

1. Why did Esther live in the home of her cousin Mordecai?
2. How did she become the queen?
3. Who was Haman, and why did he plan to kill the Jews?

4. What was Mordecai's plan to save them?
5. Why was Esther afraid to go to the king?
6. Do you think Mordecai was proud of Esther? Give reasons.
7. Can God use you in some special way?

God's Heroes

Daniel 1

What do you think of when you hear the word "hero"? Of loyalty and courage, of course! But do you know where the word comes from?

It goes back to a Greek myth or story about a beautiful girl who lived in a tower on a cliff beside a narrow, deep sea called the Hellespont.

On the other side of the narrow sea lived a young man by the name of Leander. He was so much in love with the beautiful girl that every night he would swim across the Hellespont, which was more than a mile across at its narrowest point, and climb the steep wall to her window. She always set a lamp in the window to guide him.

One night when Leander was on his way, a terrific storm came up, and he didn't make it across the sea. The next morning his sweetheart found his body on the shore. So heartbroken was she that she threw herself into the sea and was drowned too. Her name was "Hero," which explains why that word makes us think of noble qualities such as devotion, loyalty, and courage.

This story is about four young men who most certainly had those qualities.

    ❧   ❧   ❧

It really took courage to say "No!" But Daniel and his three friends had decided they couldn't obey the command of the officer in charge of the royal school.

The school was in the land of Babylon, ruled by a powerful king by the name of Nebuchadnezzar. The Babylonians were a warlike people who had overrun the land of Canaan and had taken many of the people of Israel as captives to their faraway land. Among the captives were Daniel and his three friends. They were fine-looking young men with bright minds, and they had been chosen to be students in the royal school so that they could serve in Nebuchadnezzar's kingdom. They were pleased at their good fortune until they heard that they would be expected to eat the rich food and drink the wine which was served at the king's table. Back in their own land, they had been taught by their parents and teachers that to do this would displease God and would also be harmful to their bodies. They believed their bodies had been given to them by God and that it was their duty to keep them strong and healthy. So they decided not to disobey their conscience.

Daniel, speaking for all of them, asked the officer who was in charge of their training not to ask them to do what was against their religion and home training.

"But," said the officer, "all the other young men will be drinking the king's wine and eating his rich food. They will say that you're odd. You will be laughed at and criticized."

"That's all right," answered Daniel. "To us it is more important to please God than to please them. We won't do something that's wrong just to be popular."

Deep down the officer admired Daniel and his friends for their faith and courage, so he said, "For ten days you may choose your own food and drink. After that, come back to me and let me see how you look."

So for ten days Daniel and his three friends drank water and ate a variety of fresh vegetables. When they reported back to the officer, he was amazed to see how well they looked and how healthy and strong they were. They looked much better than the other students who were eating the king's rich food and drinking his wine.

In fact, the officer was so impressed by Daniel and his friends that he permitted them to continue their special diets.

Later they graduated from the royal school and were presented to the king. They had been such good students and had taken such good care of their health that Nebuchadnezzar, as he talked with them, found them to be the most brilliant and most handsome in the entire graduating class.

He was so pleased with them that, although they were from a foreign nation, he put them in places of high honor in his kingdom.

God was pleased too, we may be sure! For isn't God always pleased with young people who take the best possible care of their bodies and minds, who have the courage to stand for what they believe is right, and who obey their conscience no matter what others may think or say?

Yes, in every age, such young people are truly "God's heroes"!

Prayer

Dear God, help me to remember in my daily life the example set by Daniel and his friends. Whenever I am tempted to do something wrong to go along with the crowd, help me to say "No" and to stand up for what I believe. In Jesus' name, amen.

Questions

1. What does the word "hero" mean?
2. Why didn't Daniel and his three friends want to eat the king's rich food and drink his wine?

3. What was the result of the ten-day test?
4. What did King Nebuchadnezzar do as a result?
5. What are some of the things to which you should say "No" today?
6. Who are some of the heroes in today's world? What makes them heroic?

Three Who Stood Up!

Daniel 3

Do you know what the word "martyr" means? Well, once it meant simply "a witness" — someone who stood up for his faith and told other people about it.

But during the early days of Christianity, there were Roman emperors who ordered Christians to be thrown to the lions or burned at the stake for claiming that Christ was their Lord. So many Christians died rather than deny their faith that the word "martyr" came to mean "one who gives his life for his faith."

This story is about three young men who were brave enough to tell a king that they would rather die than disobey God.

❧   ❧   ❧

These three young men were the same ones who, along with their friend, Daniel, had graduated with honor from the royal school in

Babylon and later had been appointed to high positions in the kingdom by King Nebuchadnezzar.

Their names were Shadrach, Meshach, and Abednego. Back in the land of Canaan they had been taught to love God and keep his commandments, and now, even though they were far away from home, they still remembered what they had been taught.

Babylon was a heathen country where the people worshiped idols rather than the true God, and Nebuchadnezzar had set up a huge idol near his palace. This idol was made of gold and was ninety feet high. One day the governors and other officials in his kingdom and the people of Babylon came together by order of the king to worship this new idol. The king gave a signal, everyone became quiet, and a herald proclaimed in a loud voice,

"You are commanded, all you people, whatever your race or country, when you hear the sound of horn, pipe, and every other kind of musical instrument, to fall to your knees and worship the golden image that King Nebuchadnezzar has set up!"

Then the herald said, even more loudly, "And if anyone does not fall down and worship the image, he shall be thrown into a fiery furnace!"

When Shadrach, Meshach, and Abednego heard this, they looked at each other and shook their heads.

"We can't do it," said Shadrach. "Remember the First Commandment we were taught years ago, back in Canaan?"

"'You shall have no other gods before me,'" said Meshach, quoting.

"And the second says almost the same thing," added Abednego.

"'You shall not make a carved image. You shall not bow down to idols or serve them, for I am the Lord your God,'" Meshach quoted again.

So, when the music was played and all the other people fell on their knees before the golden image, Shadrach, Meshach, and Abednego stood straight up. They did not so much as bow their heads.

When Nebuchadnezzar was told about this, he was very angry. He ordered the three men to be brought to him.

"Why have you disobeyed my command?" he asked.

"Because," they answered, "we worship the true God, and we have been taught that it is wrong to bow down before idols."

"And do you think your God is able to keep you from being burnt up in the fiery furnace?" asked the king.

"We are sure he is able to do that," they replied. "And we believe he will save us. But even if he allows us to die in the fire, we will not worship the gods of Babylon or bow before the golden image!"

These brave words made the king furious. He ordered his servants to heat the furnace seven times hotter than ever before. Then Shadrach, Meshach, and Abednego were tied hand and foot and thrown into the fire. The flames were so fierce that the men who threw the three believers into the fire were killed.

As the king looked through the door into the furnace, he saw a strange sight.

"Look!" he cried. "Didn't we throw three men into the fire?"

"Yes," his servants answered, "three men."

"But I see *four*," Nebuchadnezzar exclaimed, "and they are all walking through the fire. Not one of them is hurt! And the fourth man looks like a son of the gods!"

Then the king came up closer and called, "Shadrach, Meshach, and Abednego, servants of the Most High God, come out!"

When they did so, the king and his men saw that their clothes and their hair hadn't even been been scorched. They didn't even smell like they had been close to flames.

You see, God had sent his angel to protect Shadrach, Meshach, and Abednego from the fire. He was the fourth man the king had seen walking with them in the furnace.

Nebuchadnezzar was amazed and humbled. "There is no god like your God," he said. "From now on, you will be free to worship him and him only. No other God could have saved you."

The king also ordered that no one in his entire kingdom should ever say anything against the God of Shadrach, Meshach, and Abednego.

How wonderful it was that God sent his angel to guard them so that they came out of the fire unharmed. But it was also wonderful that these men had the courage to stand up for their faith and say to the king, "Even if our God does not save us, we will not worship your idols or bow before the golden image you have set up!"

Prayer

Dear God, give me the courage to stand up for my faith, no matter what others may say or do. Help me to be true to you, and true to what I believe. In Jesus' name, amen.

Questions

1. What two commandments would Shadrach, Meshach, and Abednego be breaking if they worshiped the golden idol? (See Exodus 20:1-4.)
2. What did they say to the king?
3. How did this make the king feel, and what did he do?
4. What did the king see when he looked into the furnace?
5. What did Nebuchadnezzar say and do when the three men came out from the furnace unharmed?
6. What lessons about faith can you learn from this story?

The Lion Tamer

Daniel 6

"Now I lay me down to sleep.
I pray the Lord my soul to keep.
God be with me through the night
And wake me in the morning light."

Did you learn that prayer when you were little? And do you still say your prayers every night?

What if you're not at home? What if you're spending the night with some of your friends, or you're away at camp? Do you say your prayers when the lights are out so no one will notice? Do you skip your prayers altogether? Or do you keep your good habit, no matter what your friends may think or say?

This is another story about Daniel and his courage. He had formed good prayer habits when he was young, and not even a king could make him change.

೪   ೪   ೪

Daniel couldn't remember how old he was when he began to pray. His father and mother had taught him to love God and to talk with him when he was a little boy.

Later, living far away from home and in a heathen country, he still made it his habit to pray three times every day. He was never too busy, even though at the time of this story he was one of three presidents who helped the new king, Darius, to rule his empire.

Daniel was such a good president that Darius planned to promote him and make him prime minister over his entire kingdom. This made the other two presidents and certain other officers jealous, and they began plotting to get rid of Daniel. They watched everything he did, but they couldn't find anything to complain about to the king.

At last they decided upon this evil scheme. They went to the king and said, "O King Darius, may you live forever! You are a great and noble ruler! You should be worshiped as a god!

"For that reason, we think you should make it a law that for thirty days no one shall offer a prayer to or make a request of any man or god except you.

"Also, your majesty, let it be stated that the law cannot be changed, and that if anyone disobeys it, he shall be thrown into the den of lions."

Flattered at being told that he was like a god, and not knowing about the plot against Daniel, Darius ordered the law to be drawn up and signed it.

When Daniel heard about the new law, he went straight to his home and knelt down to pray. And he didn't try to hide what he was doing! He prayed with his windows open toward Jerusalem, the city in his homeland where the temple was located.

Of course his enemies were watching, and when they saw him on his knees, they ran to the king. They told him what they had seen, and they demanded that Daniel be thrown into the den of lions.

Now the king admired Daniel so much that he was very sorry that he had signed the law, and after he heard the bad news he worked all day to see if he could avoid punishing Daniel. But according to the custom of those times, the law couldn't be changed.

When Daniel was brought before him, he told Daniel how sorry he was and added, "May your God, to whom you pray and whom you serve so faithfully, deliver you." Then Daniel was thrown into the den of lions, and a huge stone was placed over the mouth of the den so he couldn't get out.

That night the king was so worried about Daniel that he couldn't eat or sleep. Very early the next morning, he hurried down to the lions' den and called, "Daniel, Daniel! Has your God been able to save you from the lions?"

And Daniel answered, "Yes, your majesty. My God sent his angel to guard me. He shut the lions' mouths, and they haven't touched me. All night long I have been kept safe because I have done no wrong."

When the king heard this, he was overjoyed. He commanded that Daniel be taken out of the lions' den. And all who saw him were amazed because he hadn't been harmed at all.

To punish Daniel's accusers, King Darius threw *them* into the lions' den. Then he published a special decree and sent it to every part of his kingdom. It read, "Peace be unto you! I make a decree that in all my royal kingdom, men shall honor the God of Daniel, because he is the living and true God."

The brave example of Daniel reminds us that the God we read about in the Bible is the one true God. It also reminds us how important it is for us to think about him and talk with him every day.

Prayer

Dear God, whenever I come to you in prayer, you always listen to me. May I, like Daniel, never be too busy to talk to you, and may I never be ashamed to be seen in prayer. Help me never to lose touch with you, and to always remember how much you love me. In Jesus' name, amen.

Questions

1. What were Daniel's prayer habits?
2. Describe the plot against him.
3. What did Daniel do when he heard about the new law?
4. What was done to him because he disobeyed the new law?
5. Why did the king hurry down to the lions' den the next morning, and what did he find?
6. What did he do after Daniel came out unharmed?
7. Have you ever been ashamed to pray?
8. Most of us pray before bedtime and in church. What are other times and places that we can talk to God?

The Grumpy Prophet
The Book of Jonah

Have you seen the Walt Disney movie about Snow White and the seven dwarfs? If you have, you'll remember that the name of one of the dwarfs was Grumpy. How would you like that for a nickname?

You wouldn't like it at all, would you? Because the name "Grumpy" makes you think of someone who complains a lot and who doesn't like people. And you wouldn't want to be that kind of person, would you?

This story is about a man whose real name was Jonah, but he might as well have been nicknamed Grumpy, because that was the kind of man he was!

❧   ❧   ❧

The most important people in the Old Testament, Bible scholars tell us, were not the kings or the priests but the prophets. So Jonah should have been pleased and honored when God singled him out and called him to be a prophet. But, as a matter of fact, he felt just the opposite!

Why? Because he didn't want to do the first thing God asked him to do.

"Go to the great city of Nineveh," God had commanded him, "and preach to the people there. Tell them how displeased I am because of their sins, and call upon them to repent. Warn them that if they do not repent and turn from their sins, their city will be destroyed."

Why didn't Jonah want to deliver that message to Nineveh? Probably because he *wanted* the city to be *destroyed!* You see, the Assyrians who lived there had, for a long time, been the enemies of Jonah's own people, the Jews. Recently they had defeated the Jews in war and had taken many of them to Nineveh as slaves. For this reason, Jonah really wanted Nineveh to be destroyed, not saved.

So, instead of doing what God had told him to do, Jonah went down to the sea, found a ship going to Tarshish, bought a ticket, and sailed away in the opposite direction from Nineveh.

But God sent a great storm upon the sea to teach Jonah that he couldn't escape from God. Huge waves pounded the ship until it was at the point of breaking to pieces. The sailors were frantic with fear. When they questioned Jonah, they found out who he was and that he was fleeing from God. "That explains the storm," they said to each other. To Jonah they said, "Now what are we going to do with you?" Jonah knew he was to blame for the storm, so he told the sailors to throw him overboard. They didn't want to do that, but the storm kept getting worse. So in the end they threw Jonah into the sea — and the storm stopped immediately.

But God didn't let Jonah drown! He sent a great fish that swallowed him whole, without hurting him. For three days and three nights, Jonah was inside the fish. That gave him plenty of time to think about how foolish he had been. During that time, he also did a lot of praying!

After three days, God caused the great fish to cough Jonah up on dry land. Then, a second time, God said to him, "Jonah, I want you to go to Nineveh and preach to the people there. Call upon them to repent and to forsake their sinful ways."

This time Jonah did as God had commanded. He traveled to Nineveh and went up and down the many streets of the huge city, shouting, "Turn from your evil ways, or in forty days Nineveh will be destroyed!"

To Jonah's amazement, the people did repent. Even the king took off his royal robe and put on a coarse brown cloak instead. He also sat in ashes as a sign of his sorrow for his sins, and he called upon his people to turn to God and to pray that he would save them.

The people did as their king commanded, and God did forgive them.

At the end of the forty days, Jonah, seeing that the city had not been destroyed, became very "grumpy" again. He was so irritated that he told God he wanted to die. Then he went and sat outside the city walls, waiting to see what would happen to Nineveh.

As he continued pouting, the sun became hotter and hotter. Once again, God treated him better than he deserved. He caused a large vine with wide leaves to grow up over Jonah's head. That protected him from the heat of the sun and made him feel better for a little while.

But the next day God caused the vine to wither, and Jonah, feeling the hot rays of the sun on his head, became "grumpy" again and complained because the vine had died. Again he became so irritated that he told God he wanted to die.

At this point God told Jonah what he thought about the way he was acting.

"Jonah," God said, "you should be ashamed of yourself! You wanted me to save the vine that sprang up and sheltered you from the heat of the sun, but you didn't want me to save Nineveh, a city of more than 120,000 people who are ignorant sinners. But Jonah, whether you like it or not, I will always be a merciful, forgiving, and loving God to those who turn from their sins and ask me to save them."

In this way God tried to teach Jonah the truth that Jesus taught his disciples years later when he said, "Everyone who calls upon the name of the Lord will be saved" (Romans 10:13).

Did Jonah finally learn this glorious truth about God? Or did he keep on being "grumpy"?

The Bible doesn't tell us. But let's hope he did. And let's hope that we have learned an important lesson from this story that we'll never forget.

Prayer

Dear God, I want to serve you happily, not to resist your will like Jonah did. I'll go where you want me to go, I'll do what you want me to do, I'll be what you want me to be. I'll tell all people how you love them, and that you want to forgive them and save them. And help me never to be grumpy, but each day to be more and more like you. In Jesus' name, amen.

Questions

1. Why was Jonah grumpy about what God wanted him to do?
2. What did Jonah do instead?
3. Then what did God do and why?
4. What did Jonah do when he was inside the great fish?
5. What did Jonah do after the fish coughed him up?
6. What did the people of Nineveh do after Jonah preached to them? What did God do?
7. Why did Jonah become "grumpy" again?
8. What lesson was God trying to teach Jonah?
9. To whom and how did Jesus teach the same lesson years later?
10. How should we feel toward "wicked" people?

No Vacancy

Luke 1:31-33; 2:1-20; Matthew 1:20-21

If you were traveling across the country with your family, where would you expect to spend the night? Perhaps in a motel?

But suppose you had car trouble, and it was after dark when you arrived in the town where you planned to stop, and the motels were all full — "No Vacancy" signs everywhere! What would you do?

Would you be willing to sleep in a barn if someone offered it to you? Perhaps you would if you were very, very tired and there was nowhere else to go.

Many years ago something like that happened to a Jewish family in a faraway country, and the day it happened has been remembered ever since!

❧   ❧   ❧

Simeon, owner of the inn in Bethlehem, had mixed feelings about the new national census ordered by the Roman emperor. It meant that people all across the land had to go to their hometowns so that the

[146]

number of people in each family could be recorded. Simeon knew the census meant higher taxes for him and for his fellow Jews throughout the land of Palestine, and he didn't like that. But it also meant more business for his inn — and that was something he did like.

For days before the census, he and his servants were busy gathering supplies. By noon on the day before the registration was to begin, most of the rooms in his inn were already taken, and people were still crowding into the city. Early in the afternoon, Simeon put up the "No Vacancy" sign — his inn was full.

Simeon was very happy about that. Most of his guests were wealthy and spent their money freely, ordering food and wine. The jingle of silver and gold coins dropping into his purse was music to Simeon's ears. Already he was one of the richest men in Bethlehem. Still, something was missing. . . .

Shortly after dark, a man and woman opened the door of the inn and came over to where Simeon sat counting his money. At a glance he saw that they were poor and very tired. Also, the woman looked as if she were in pain.

It was the man who spoke: "My name is Joseph, and this is my wife, Mary. We have come from Nazareth in Galilee to register in the census. We need lodging for the night."

"Sorry," Simeon replied, "my rooms are all taken. Surely you saw the 'No Vacancy' sign on the door!"

"It's urgent," Joseph pleaded. "Please don't turn us away. My wife is exhausted, and tonight her baby may be born!"

A woman about to have a baby! That was the last thing Simeon wanted at a time like this. The struggle with his conscience was short. "My good man, I'm very sorry. But as I've already said, my inn is full!" And he stood up to indicate the conversation was over.

But the conversation wasn't over! Just then, the woman, pale and weary, fainted into her husband's arms. Gently he laid her on the floor, pulling off his cloak to make a pillow for her head.

As Simeon looked down at her pale but beautiful face, his heart was troubled. "My friend," he said to Joseph, "behind the inn is a cave used as a stable. The first stall is empty, with fresh, clean straw. You may spend the night there, if you wish." Mary was reviving. With a tear in her eye, she whispered, "Oh, thank you." Simeon had to turn his eyes away. He ordered a servant to show them to the stable and told him to get them a candle, a pitcher of water, and some food. Then he turned to take care of his guests, who were calling loudly for more wine.

It was almost midnight when he went up to bed. The back window of his room opened out toward the stable. He noticed that a light was still burning in the first stall. He wondered about the woman and whether or not the baby had arrived.

But why should he be concerned? He had his other guests to think about — his *paying* guests! He couldn't be responsible for every expectant mother and every newborn baby in the world! Shrugging his shoulders, he threw himself on his bed. Soon he was fast asleep.

Two or three hours later he was awakened by the sound of voices coming from the direction of the stable. Fearing that the guests in his inn might be disturbed, he threw a cloak over his shoulders and rushed out.

To his amazement, he found a number of shepherds crowding into the stable to see the newborn baby. Joseph and Mary were listening intently as the shepherds told why they had come.

"We were out under the stars guarding our sheep. Suddenly a company of angels appeared in the sky. They were singing, 'Glory to God in the highest.' One of the angels said, 'This day, in the city of

David, a Savior is born who is Christ the Lord. And this is the sign that will guide you: you will find the baby wrapped in cloths and lying in a manger.' So we came as fast as we could."

As Simeon listened to that amazing story and looked down into the face of the newborn baby, his heart melted. He had come to drive the shepherds away. Now he felt as they did!

But why hadn't the angel come to him? Had he known that the baby was to be the Savior of the world, he would have found room for Joseph and Mary in the inn. He would have given them his own room.

Was it because he had been too busy thinking about money and trying to make more and more of it? Was it because he hadn't found time to look at the stars or to think about God or the angels, or about how much the world needed a Savior?

After the shepherds left, Simeon spoke kindly to Joseph and Mary. He asked for their forgiveness and invited them to come back to the inn and take his room. "I can sleep on a couch in the hall," he said. "I should have thought of that before."

Joseph assured Simeon he was forgiven but declined his invitation. "My wife isn't strong enough to walk yet," he said. "We're all right here. As you said, the stable is clean, and the hay in the manger is fresh. And the baby's already asleep."

"He is truly a beautiful child," said Simeon. "Have you decided on his name?"

"God made that decision for us," replied Joseph. "Several months ago, an angel appeared to me, and also to Mary at a different time, and said, 'You shall call him Jesus [which means "Savior"] because he will save his people from their sins.'"

Joseph's words spoke straight to the greatest need in Simeon's life. So Simeon stepped over to the manger where the baby Jesus was sleeping and, bowing his head, asked God to forgive him for his selfishness and unkindness in sending Joseph and Mary out to the stable, and to forgive him for all his other sins too. Then he said to the three of them, "Good night and God bless you," and left.

Somehow, as he went up to his room and to bed, his conscience wasn't troubling him anymore. His heart was filled with great joy.

Prayer

Dear God, please don't let my heart be like Simeon's inn — a place that has no room for you. Help me always to cherish Christ's birth, and all the things he has done for me. In Jesus' name, amen.

Questions

1. How did Simeon feel about the new census? Why?
2. What was it like at the inn on the day before the census?
3. Who were the travelers who arrived late and asked for a room?
4. Who was the baby born that night? How did he get his name? What does his name mean?
5. If you have guests at home and they spend the night, how do you feel about giving up your bed for them? Why do you suppose Simeon didn't offer his bed to Mary and Joseph until later?
6. Why do you think the angels told the shepherds about Jesus, but didn't tell Simeon?
7. What do you think Simeon did differently at his inn after he met Jesus?
8. How can you be less selfish?

A Star Is Born

Matthew 2:1-12

Have you ever looked up into the sky, picked out one of the stars as if it belonged to you, and repeated this rhyme?

> Twinkle, twinkle, little star,
> How I wonder what you are,
> Up above the world so high,
> Like a diamond in the sky.

In the Bible there's a story about a very special star. We don't know whether it twinkled or not. But the Bible tells us it moved, and some men who were said to be very wise followed it for days and days — or maybe I should say nights and nights — until it led them to . . . But let's not run ahead of the story.

❧   ❧   ❧

Several miles outside the city of Jerusalem, three friends stood, each beside his camel, gazing into the night sky. Their names were Caspar, Balthasar, and Melchior, and they were troubled because, while the sky was bright with stars, they couldn't find the one they were looking for.

"Strange that it should lead us this far and then disappear," said Caspar.

"Perhaps this is God's way of telling us that we're almost there," Balthasar added. "Maybe Jerusalem is the place. That's where one would expect a new king of the Jews to be born."

The three men were silent for a moment, then Melchior said, "Tomorrow we can go into the city and ask whether anyone knows about the birth of a new prince."

Caspar, Balthasar, and Melchior were not only friends but men who studied the stars very carefully. For this reason they were known as "Magi," or "wise men." Back in Persia, the land from which they had come, they had often discussed with Hebrew scholars certain passages in the Hebrew Scriptures where prophets had spoken of a king who would someday come and bring justice and peace to the world. There was one prophecy in particular that connected this king's coming with the appearance of a new star. It read, "I see him, but not now; I behold him, but not near. A star will come out of Jacob; a scepter will rise out of Israel" (Numbers 24:17, NIV).

The three wise men had come to believe that the new star they had discovered in the sky was the very one that the Hebrew prophecy was speaking about. So they had left their native land of Persia and for several weeks had followed the star as it moved across the sky.

They had sold many of their possessions in order to buy a train of camels and supplies for the journey. Also, each of them had purchased a rich present to give to the newborn king, if and when they should find him.

They had come several hundred miles, and they were very tired.

But the appearance of the star every night had kept their hopes alive — that is, until now, when it wasn't to be seen anywhere.

Before the wise men entered Jerusalem the next morning, King Herod's spies had already reported their presence outside the city. The wise men made a very impressive sight as they rode in on their colorfully decorated camels. They created a great deal of curiosity as they went here and there asking people, "Where is the one who has been born king of the Jews? We have seen his star in the East and have come to worship him."

When Herod heard that, he knew it was time to act. He couldn't stand the thought of anyone besides himself being king!

Immediately he summoned the Jewish religious scholars in the city and passed the Magi's question on to them. They quickly came up with the answer.

"He will be born in Bethlehem of Judea," they said, "for this is what the prophet Micah wrote: 'O little town of Bethlehem, you are not just an insignificant Jewish village. For from you shall come a ruler who will govern my people Israel.'"

Then Herod was really troubled! Sending away the religious scholars, he said to himself, "I am king, and I intend to remain king! No newborn baby in Bethlehem or anywhere else will get my throne!"

Covering up his fear and jealousy, he pretended to be friendly toward the Magi and invited them to his palace. His invitation brought them a new spark of hope — "Maybe the newborn prince is Herod's son," they said to one another. This certainly wasn't the case. Herod's sons were grown men and as unworthy to be king as Herod was. Of course the Magi didn't know this yet.

So when they were ushered into Herod's presence, they told him about the star and asked him whether he knew where the new king the Hebrew prophets had spoken about was to be born. "We have come from far away to worship him," they said.

Herod, pretending to be friendly, said in a smooth voice, "When did this new star you have been following first appear?"

"Many nights ago, when we were still in Persia," they answered.

"And where is it now?" he asked.

"We don't know," they replied.

"Then go on to Bethlehem," Herod said cunningly. "According to our scholars, that is where he is to be born. Keep searching for the young child until you find him, and when you do, come back and report to me, and I will go and worship him, too."

The Magi didn't know that Herod in his evil heart was already planning to kill the baby. It wasn't worship that he had in mind, but murder!

After the wise men left the palace, they took the road to Bethlehem. Suddenly, there was the star again, going on before them! Their joy knew no bounds as they followed it on and on until it stopped above the very house where the baby Jesus was.

When they entered, they saw ordinary people: a carpenter whose name was Joseph, and his wife, Mary, and a sweet little child in her arms. But they knew this was the child they were seeking because the star that had led them all the way from Persia kept shining right above the house where they were! So they fell on their knees in worship and thanked God for having guided them all the way.

Then, going out to their camels, they unloaded the costly gifts they had brought and placed them in front of the baby. Caspar's gift was gold. Balthasar's was frankincense, which was burned for its fragrance. Melchior's was sweet-smelling myrrh, a rich ointment.

Perhaps you're thinking, "What strange gifts to bring to a little baby!" And you're right. But, you see, Jesus was a very special baby. And through those gifts God was revealing who Jesus was and why he had been sent into the world. The gold was a sign that he would someday be a king and that we should obey him. The frankincense was a sign that he was divine, God's own Son, and that we should worship him. And the myrrh was a sign that he would later die on a cross to save us from our sins.

Seen this way, the presents the wise men brought were not strange gifts after all, but most appropriate, indicating who Jesus was and why God sent him into the world. So we, like Mary and Joseph, should be grateful for the gifts the wise men chose and brought to the baby Jesus many long years ago.

Prayer

Dear God, when I hear the story of the wise men, my first thought may be that I have no expensive gift for Jesus — no gold or frankincense or myrrh. But help me to remember that I have the most important gift of all to give him — my heart. In Jesus' name, amen.

Questions

1. Why were the wise men troubled at the beginning of the story?
2. Why were they following a star?
3. What did they keep asking people the next morning in Jerusalem?

4. What would you think about three strangers in your town asking about a newborn king?
5. Why did Herod say he invited the wise men to his palace? What was his real reason?
6. What do you think about Herod's jealousy? What makes you jealous? How can you change that?
7. What gifts did the wise men bring Jesus? What did they mean?
8. What do you suppose the wise men thought when they discovered that the "King" they were looking for was in the home of a poor carpenter? What do you think their reaction teaches us?
9. What is the best gift you can bring to Jesus?

Mixed Blessings

Matthew 2:12-21; Luke 2:22-40

Sometimes we say that a certain experience is a "mixed blessing." By that we mean that it has both a bright side and a dark side.

For example, when you were born, you were a "mixed blessing" to your parents.

On the bright side, they had new reasons for joy — your rosy little face, your sweet smile, the congratulations and good wishes of friends, and their hopes and dreams about your future.

But they had new concerns too — concerns about your health and your safety and, as you grew older, concerns about your education, your friends, your habits, and your faith.

This same thing was true about the birth of Jesus. At the beginning, it was joy upon joy for Mary and Joseph.

But concerns were not long in coming.

❧   ❧   ❧

When the wise men visited Herod the king, he asked them to come back to Jerusalem after they had found the newborn baby and tell him where the child was. Although he said he wanted to come and worship the child, he really wanted to kill the baby. So God warned the Magi about Herod's plot, and they went back to their own country by another route.

Herod was furious when he found this out. He ordered his soldiers to go to Bethlehem and the surrounding area and do something extreme: to kill every baby boy who was two years old and younger.

What a cruel thing for Herod to do! But that was his way of making sure that no newborn baby would ever become king and replace him. Or so he thought. In the meantime, an angel had appeared to Joseph in a dream.

"Get up quickly," the angel said. "Take the child and his mother, and flee to the land of Egypt, for Herod is planning to search for the child and kill him."

So Joseph woke Mary up and told her about the dream. They hurried to get ready to leave. When they were ready, they picked up the baby Jesus and slipped away in the middle of the night.

The next day, Herod's soldiers came to Bethlehem and obeyed Herod's command. They killed all the tiny baby boys. That was a very sad day for all the people in the town.

But Jesus was already on his way to the land of Egypt. There he and Mary and Joseph lived until the wicked Herod died. Then an angel appeared to Joseph in another dream and told him it was now safe for the family to return to their own country.

So they set out from Egypt to go home again. To them, home was a village called Nazareth in Galilee, about sixty miles north of Jerusalem.

On the way home, coming up from the land of Egypt, Mary said to Joseph, "We must stop in Jerusalem and go to the temple. There we will give thanks for Jesus and dedicate him to God."

So they did. And while they were there, an old man named Simeon came in. He was a good man and very religious. He knew all about God's promise to send to the world a great King and Savior called the Messiah. The Holy Spirit had revealed to Simeon that he would not die until he had seen this promised Savior. When Simeon saw Mary and Joseph and the baby Jesus, the Holy Spirit whispered to him again, "This is the child that will become God's Messiah."

After hearing the Spirit's message, Simeon hurried over to Mary and Joseph. He asked if he might hold Jesus in his arms. Then he prayed, "Dear God, thank you for this moment. Now I'm ready to die because I have seen with my own eyes the Savior you have sent to bring light and peace to all the people."

Then he blessed Mary and Joseph. He told them that to be the Savior of the world, Jesus would later have to suffer many things. While many people would love him, others would hate him and try to kill him.

Then, turning to Mary, Simeon said, "Later you too will be called upon to suffer as if a sword had pierced your own heart." At the time, Mary didn't know what Simeon meant, but she didn't forget his words. She understood what he meant later, when Jesus was crucified.

At that moment a very religious woman, known as a prophetess, came over to where they were standing. Anna was her name, and she was eighty-four years old. When she saw Jesus, she also took him into her arms and thanked God. Then she announced to others nearby in the temple that this child would be the Messiah of the nation and the Savior of the world.

Both Simeon and Anna praised God with deep joy and gratitude in their hearts. Mary and Joseph were happy and grateful too, because the words of these two special believers had reminded them of what the shepherds and the Magi had said when Jesus was born.

As they left the temple, Joseph said to Mary, "God has truly blessed us with a very special little son! Let's continue to pray that he will grow up to be the kind of Savior the world needs."

"And when we get home," Mary added, "we must do our part to teach him all the things he will need to know in order to be able to do all that God expects of him."

With this purpose in their hearts, the next morning they started out again for their home in Nazareth. There Jesus continued to grow stronger and wiser day after day in a way that pleased God very much.

Prayer

Dear God, thank you for everyone who loved me and said nice things about me when I was a little baby. Help me to be the kind of boy or girl that they will love and say nice things about as I grow older. Help me to be what you want me to be. In Jesus' name, amen.

Questions

1. In what way were you a "mixed blessing" to your parents when you were born?
2. Why did the wise men not visit Jerusalem on their way back to their country?
3. What did Herod do when he found out what they had done?
4. What did the angel tell Joseph to do?
5. On their way back from Egypt, what did Mary and Joseph do in Jerusalem?
6. What did Simeon do and say when he saw the baby Jesus?
7. What did Anna do and say?
8. How do you suppose Mary felt about Simeon's words about Jesus and about her? What do you think Joseph thought?
9. How do you suppose the other people in the temple felt about what Simeon and Anna said about Jesus?

Questions and Answers

Luke 2:41-52

When you have questions that puzzle or trouble you — about God, about the Bible, about what is right and what is wrong, about what to do with your life — where do you go for answers? To your father or mother? To one of your teachers? To the minister of your church?

When Jesus was a boy, where do you suppose he went for the answers to such questions?

❧   ❧   ❧

Jesus was almost too excited to sleep! All day long he had helped his mother and father get together the things they would need for their journey the next day. They were going to Jerusalem to celebrate the Passover.

The Passover was a religious festival observed by Jewish families once every year. It was an expression of their thanksgiving to God for delivering them from slavery in the land of Egypt many years before.

[164]

Mary and Joseph went to Jerusalem every year for this celebration. Jesus was now twelve years old, so for the first time he was going too.

To Jerusalem! To worship God in his holy temple! The temple he had heard so much about in the synagogue school. The temple, where, as he had been told, his parents had taken him when he was a baby and dedicated him to God. The temple, where there were brilliant religious teachers who would be able to answer some of the questions that kept coming to his mind. No wonder Jesus was excited!

The next morning, with Mary and Joseph, he was up bright and early to start on the journey. There were many people going from Nazareth. They traveled together in what was called a caravan. They walked all day, sharing their food along the way, and they slept at night under the stars. Jerusalem was about sixty miles from Nazareth, and since they were traveling on foot, it took them three or four days to make the journey. When they stopped and made camp for the last night, they could see the walls of the city and the temple on the hills above them.

After supper, the people gathered for an evening worship service. Facing toward the temple, they sang one of their familiar psalms:

> I to the hills will lift mine eyes,
> O whence for me shall help arise?
> From the Lord shall come my aid,
> Who the heaven and earth hath made.
>
> He will surely keep thy soul,
> What would harm he will control.
> He will keep thee day by day,
> In the home and by the way.

The next morning, as the people entered the temple courtyard, Jesus was fascinated but troubled by what he saw. Money changers were everywhere, shouting to get attention and overcharging people as they exchanged Roman coins for Jewish money. Merchants were asking three times too much for the doves and lambs required for the sacrificial offerings! All around were priests, hundreds of them, living on the gifts the people brought to the temple.

When Jesus saw these things, his mind began to spin with questions. Why did the merchants charge so much for the animals? What did the priests do with the money? Why did they sacrifice animals on the altar? Was this all God expected and wanted of people? Weren't there other things that were more important? What did God want most of all?

Jesus recalled some of the verses from the prophets he had heard and memorized in the synagogue school. He remembered a particular verse from Isaiah: "'The multitude of your sacrifices — what are they to me?' says the Lord. 'I have more than enough of burnt offerings, of rams and the fat of fattened animals; I have no pleasure in the blood of bulls and lambs and goats'" (1:11, NIV).

And Jesus remembered another verse from Micah: "He has showed you, O man, what is good. And what does the Lord require of you? To act justly and to love mercy and to walk humbly with your God" (6:8, NIV).

Jesus wondered whether the prophets were right. If they were, why were all these animals being sacrificed on the altar? What was the heart of religion, the most important thing about it?

These were some of the questions that kept going around in Jesus' mind as he watched what was going on in the temple. He needed to know the answers if he was someday to be God's Messiah! And this should be the place and the time to get the answers — for wasn't this God's house, his heavenly Father's house? The questions lingered in his mind that night as he tried to sleep with the other people from Nazareth in the camp they had pitched outside of Jerusalem.

The next morning the group decided that they would go back to the temple for one more worship service and then start for home. Later that morning, Jesus noticed a group of priests and religious teachers in a balcony of the temple. They were consulting the Scriptures and were discussing and debating certain passages from the prophets. "Perhaps here I could find the answers to some of my questions," Jesus thought to himself. Turning away from the crowd moving into the worship service, he joined the discussion group. He listened eagerly to everything that was being said. When he had a chance, he began asking questions himself.

The learned doctors of religion were amazed that a boy so young could come up with such intelligent questions. They were also amazed by the answers he gave to some of their questions. On and on the discussion went, with both Jesus and the teachers so interested that they lost all sense of time.

It was very late when they finally stopped the discussion. Jesus slept alone in the temple so he could return early to the discussion the next day. He spent that whole day again discussing the Scriptures with the priests and teachers. For a second night he slept alone in the temple. On the third day, while Jesus was again involved in a discussion of the Scriptures with the temple scholars, Mary and Joseph rushed into the temple.

Throwing her arms around Jesus, Mary said with tears in her eyes, "Oh, my son, we thought you were lost! We've been looking everywhere for you! We thought you were with some of our friends and relatives,

but when we couldn't find you anywhere in the group returning to Nazareth, we came all the way back to look for you. Why did you treat us this way?"

Jesus was sorry about his mother's anxiety, but he was glad he had stayed to get the answers to some of his questions. So he said,

"Why did you look for me somewhere else, Mother? Didn't you know I would be here in my Father's house learning about my Father's business?"

Mary didn't understand this strange answer at the time. But she kept thinking about it. The more she did, the more she realized that even at the age of twelve, Jesus was well on the way to becoming what God, his heavenly Father, had sent him into the world to be — the promised Messiah and Savior of the world!

After that never-to-be-forgotten experience in the temple, Jesus went back to Nazareth with Mary and Joseph. There, through his teenage years, he continued to live as their dutiful son — working, studying, listening, learning, and all the while thinking and praying more and more about his "heavenly Father's business."

He was loved and admired by all who knew him. And in due time, he was fully prepared to fulfill the purpose for which God had sent him into the world.

Prayer

Dear God, I want to follow the example of Jesus in this story. I want to find and to fulfill the purpose you had in mind when you sent me into the world. I want to be the person you want me to be and to do the work you want me to do.

So help me to use my time, my opportunities, and my talents while I am growing up so that I too may be fully prepared for what you want me to be and to do when I am fully grown. In Jesus' name, amen.

Questions

1. Why was the Passover celebration so important to Jewish families during Jesus' time?
2. Why was Jesus eager to visit the temple in Jerusalem?
3. What did Jesus see the people doing in the temple courtyard? Why was he troubled?
4. Why did the Jews offer sacrifices? What do you think the words of the prophets meant?
5. What did Jesus do about the questions he had? What did the religious teachers think about him?
6. How do you feel about asking questions? Whom do you go to when you want to know something about the Bible?
7. What do you think of how Mary reacted when she and Joseph found Jesus in the temple?
8. What do you think Jesus meant when he answered Mary? What is God's business?

Doing God's Will

Matthew 3; Luke 3:1-18, 21-22; John 1:29-34

Some young people leave home because they get fed up with parents and other adults telling them what to do; they want to be on their own and make their own decisions. In the Bible there's a story about a young man who left home because he "looked up" and decided he wanted to do what his Father in heaven wanted him to do.

❧   ❧   ❧

As you may recall, when Jesus was twelve years old, he went with Mary and Joseph to Jerusalem for the Passover celebration. After his unforgettable experience in the temple there, he spent the next eighteen years of his life in Nazareth. There, day after day, he worked with Joseph in the carpenter shop and in this way helped to support the family. There were several younger children in the family besides Jesus, so it helped to have two men working to support them.

When Jesus was thirty years old, he realized that the time had come for him to move out into the world and to tend to his "heavenly Father's business."

Then he thought of his cousin, John, known as John the Baptist. Jesus knew that God had sent John to prepare the people for his own coming. So he decided to go to John to be baptized.

In some ways John was a strange man. He lived in a cave in the desert. His hair and beard were long. His regular diet was locusts and wild honey. The clothing he wore was a rough cloak made from the hide of a camel, with a leather belt tied around his waist.

But he was really a powerful preacher! His eyes flashed like flames of fire, and his voice was deep like the roll of thunder as he shouted, "Repent! Turn away from your sins! For the kingdom of heaven is near, and God's Messiah is coming soon."

Up and down near the river Jordan he went, preaching to the crowds of people who came. And they did come, from miles around, to see him and to hear what he had to say.

People listened, spellbound, to his words, and hundreds confessed their sins and were baptized by him in the river Jordan. They were so impressed by his eloquence and by the multitudes that followed him that some of them said to each other, "Perhaps this man is the Messiah."

But John said, "No! After me is coming one much greater than I. I am only a voice crying in the wilderness. I am the one Isaiah the prophet was speaking about when he wrote, 'Prepare the way for the Lord. Make a straight path for his coming.' The one God is sending is so much greater than I that I'm not even worthy to stoop down to untie his sandals. I can only baptize with water, but he will baptize with the Holy Spirit."

But while John was sure that the Messiah was about to come and that he would be a very great man, he didn't know who the Messiah was going to be. So he prayed for God to give him a sign. God's answer was this: "When you see the Holy Spirit coming down from heaven in the form of a dove and resting upon a man, that is the Messiah."

Not long after that, Jesus came to the river Jordan and asked John to baptize him. When John saw him coming, he recognized him

immediately — that is, he recognized Jesus as his cousin. Although the two had grown up in homes about sixty miles apart — which in those days was a long distance — they had sometimes met at Passover time in Jerusalem or at a family reunion, so they knew each other. And now, as Jesus came nearer, the Holy Spirit whispered to John, "This is the Lamb of God. He will take away the sins of the world."

In an instant, John realized that God had sent Jesus to be the Savior and the Messiah. So he said to Jesus, "I am not worthy to baptize you; it should be the other way around. You should baptize me."

But Jesus replied, "No, John, this is the way it should be. I want to show that I approve of the message you preach and that people are doing the right thing when they turn away from their sins and are baptized."

Then the two men went down to the river together, and John did baptize Jesus. After they came up out of the water and Jesus was kneeling on the bank praying, John received the sign God had promised: the Holy Spirit came down from heaven in the form of a dove and rested on Jesus' shoulder. John saw it clearly, and then he knew for certain that Jesus was the Messiah whom God had promised.

But that wasn't all that happened while Jesus was praying. A voice also came down from heaven, saying, "You are my own dear Son, and I am greatly pleased with you."

Those words were spoken to encourage Jesus and to make him strong in the face of the trials and temptations that lay ahead. In other words, God was saying, "So far, so good, my dear Son. You have made a good beginning and have made me very happy. Carry on! Carry on!"

Prayer

Dear God, help me to resist the temptation to do what I want to do without regard for your will. Help this to be my prayer and promise:

> I'll go where you want me to go,
> O'er mountain, or plain, or sea;
> I'll do what you want me to do,
> I'll be what you want me to be.
> Just as I am — young, strong, and free;
> To be the best that I can be
> For truth and righteousness and Thee,
> Lord of my life, I come.

In Jesus' name, amen.

Questions

1. Why did Jesus decide to leave his home in Nazareth? How old was he then?
2. What was the first thing he did after leaving home?
3. Describe John the Baptist.
4. What did he say to people who thought he might be the Messiah?
5. What sign did God promise to give him about the Messiah?
6. What did John say when Jesus asked to be baptized?
7. What was Jesus' reply?

8. Describe what happened after Jesus was baptized.
9. If God spoke to you the way he did to Jesus, would he say he was pleased or unhappy? What can you do to please God?

The Little Lunch That Went a Long Way

John 6:1-14

Perhaps you've heard the fable about the lion caught in a trap. The hunters who trapped him planned to carry him to the king, so they bound him tightly with a rope, tied him to a tree, and went to get a wagon.

While they were gone, along came the mouse who was a friend of the lion. With his sharp teeth, the mouse gnawed and gnawed on the rope until it broke in two, and the lion was set free!

This fable reminds us that a person doesn't have to be big to do something important. There's a story in the Bible which tells us that, too.

❧   ❧   ❧

The dust and sand went sailing through the door as Rachel vigorously pushed her reed broom over the floor of her modest home on the side

[177]

of the hill close to the Sea of Galilee. Already she had pulled aside the curtain hanging over the window to let in the light of the sun.

Her husband, Daniel, who was a carpenter, had left for work an hour earlier. But first he had helped their six-year-old son, Joel, put together his simple fishing equipment. Joel and two of his little friends had often "tried their luck" from the dock at the foot of the hill, and today they were going again. Rachel had packed him a little lunch and sent him on his joyful way just a few minutes ago. She had smiled as she watched him go down the path, clutching his fishing rod in one hand and his lunch bag in the other.

"Be careful," she had called. "Remember to stay on the dock, and don't forget we want some nice fresh fish for supper." She and Daniel knew the lake well. When they had been little, they had often played on the sandy shore and waded in its cool, shallow water.

Both of them were proud of their son — his healthy body, his bright mind, his dancing brown eyes, his mop of curly brown hair. And they enjoyed him: through Joel's happy, carefree spirit, they were reliving their own childhood. Their one concern was that now and then as he played with his friends, he seemed selfish and inconsiderate, unwilling to share, greedy. "But he'll outgrow that," they said to each other, and they hoped and prayed that it would be true.

Soon after she had finished putting her house in order, Rachel picked up her water jar and headed for the village well. There she met two of her friends, Deborah and Miriam, who had also come to draw water. As they filled their jars, they shared news about their village and the outside world. On this particular morning, Deborah could hardly wait to share her big piece of news.

"Last night, my husband heard through a fisherman friend whose name is Zebedee that the famous teacher, Jesus from Nazareth, is on the other side of the lake with a great crowd following him. Two of his twelve disciples are sons of Zebedee, and they think he may come over to our side of the lake sometime today."

"But why would he come over to our little village?" asked Miriam. "There are so many more people on the other side of the lake."

"That's just the reason," answered Deborah. "According to Zebedee, over there the crowds are so large that he needs to rest."

"It sounds too good to be true," said Rachel, her eyes bright with expectation. Then she thought of Daniel. The house he was helping to build was close to theirs, but higher on the hill. From that point he would be able to see far out onto the lake and watch for any boat that might be approaching. So Rachel told her friends she would go and tell her husband to watch for Jesus. Eager to see what would happen, the three women picked up their water jars and hurried home.

Daniel was also excited by the news Rachel reported, and he promised to keep watching the lake. But he said he didn't think any teacher as famous as Jesus of Nazareth would ever visit their little village.

Before long, Deborah's report was the biggest topic of conversation all over town. Excitement and hope were spreading like wildfire!

Just before noon, Daniel came down from the hill and reported, first to Rachel and then to the townspeople, that he had seen a boat coming across the lake. "And from the top of the hill," he said excitedly, "I saw a big crowd walking around the lake, coming this way. Lots of the people on the other side of the lake seem to be following Jesus over here."

Soon the whole village was on the move as men, women, and children hurried down to the dock where the boat was pulling in. Shouts of welcome were heard as Jesus, followed by his twelve disciples, stepped ashore. Two of the recognized leaders of the community greeted them warmly and asked Jesus to stay and teach the people as he had

taught those on the other side of the lake. So Jesus, although he was quite tired, invited the people to follow him up the hill. There he would teach them.

As Rachel and Daniel walked up the hill together, she suddenly thought of Joel. "Where do you suppose he is?" she said to Daniel. "The boat tied up at the same dock where he was supposed to be fishing, but I didn't see him anywhere."

"Don't worry," Daniel answered. "He's good at taking care of himself. Besides, everybody in the village knows him. He'll be all right."

By the time Jesus began to teach, the crowd had grown to several thousand because of the hundreds of people who had walked around the lake from the other side. And how intently they all listened! Never had they heard such words before!

Jesus spoke about God's loving care: "Look at the birds flying and singing in the blue sky. God takes care of them, and you mean more to him than they do. So don't worry about anything. Trust your heavenly Father, and he will supply all your needs."

And he spoke about faith and prayer: "Ask and you will receive; seek and you will find; knock and the door will open. If those of you who are parents find joy in giving good gifts to your children, surely your Father in heaven will not fail to give good gifts to you, his children, if you ask him."

And he spoke about unselfishness and love: "Treat others as you want them to treat you. Remember, there is more joy in giving than in receiving."

Jesus had been speaking for nearly an hour when suddenly Daniel and Rachel spied Joel. He was standing not far from Jesus. In fact, he was right beside one of Jesus' disciples. His fishing rod was on the ground beside him, and at his feet was his lunch bag. Apparently he had become so excited that he had forgotten about his lunch.

Joel's eyes were fixed on Jesus. He was drinking in every word as Jesus said, "Come to me, all of you who are tired and who carry heavy burdens, and I will give you rest. Bring to me your little children, too, that I may bless them. For to them belongs the kingdom of God. I say to you, anyone who does not come to God with the loving trust of a little child will not enter God's kingdom."

By now it was getting late, and Jesus was coming to the close of his message. As he finished, he blessed the people in God's name. As the people lingered, they could see that he was talking quietly with his disciples.

Then one of them, the one who had been beside Joel — his name was Andrew — stepped forward and announced, "Our Master knows that you're hungry, and he wants you to have something to eat before you go home. Do you have any food you would be willing to share with each other?"

The people looked at each other in amazement. What a strange request! Way out here on the hillside in late afternoon — who could possibly have any food?

But, unnoticed by anyone except his father and mother and a few people close to Andrew, Joel was stepping forward. Holding out his bag to Andrew, he said, "Here's my lunch. I'll share it with someone."

"Well, well, my little man," said Andrew, "how generous of you! Let's see what's inside." Then, looking into the bag, he said, "Not a very big lunch, is it? But let's take it to Jesus."

So they walked over to where Jesus was standing. "Master," said Andrew, "this little boy has brought his lunch — five barley rolls and two little fish. He wants to share it, but, of course, it couldn't begin to feed this crowd."

"Andrew," replied Jesus, "you must not forget that with God all things are possible. Have the people sit down."

As Andrew and the other disciples did as Jesus said, Jesus took the lunch from Joel. He thanked Joel for sharing it, and he asked God to bless it and to make it enough so all the people could eat. After his prayer, Jesus began to break the rolls and fish into small pieces and to pass them to his disciples. They in turn shared with the people, who passed the food among one another. The more they shared, the more there was to share.

Finally, all of the people had eaten as much as they wanted — and there was still food to spare! Twelve baskets of bread crusts were left from the barley loaves. When the people saw this, they realized that they had witnessed a miracle. "This is the prophet we have been promised!" they exclaimed.

Not one person went away hungry — not even Joel, because he too had eaten as much as he wanted. And he was happier than he had ever been before! Why? Because he had learned from his own experience the truth of that common saying: "There is more joy in giving than in receiving."

Prayer

Dear God, I live in a world that often encourages me to put myself first. Help me to remember that I'm never truly happy when I'm selfish. So whether I have a lot or a little, teach me the joy of sharing. In Jesus' name, amen.

Questions

1. What was Daniel and Rachel's one concern about Joel?
2. Why did Jesus go from one side of the lake to the other?
3. What are some of the things Joel heard Jesus say?
4. What did Joel do when Andrew asked whether anyone had some food to share?
5. What do you suppose Joel thought when he offered his lunch to Andrew?
6. What do you think he thought after Jesus fed all those people with his lunch?
7. Have you ever felt you weren't important because you were small? What have you learned from this story about that?
8. What do you think Joel learned about selfishness? What have you learned about selfishness?

Standing Tall

Luke 19:1-10

Are you familiar with the expression "standing tall"? It doesn't really have anything to do with how tall you are; it has to do with how you feel about yourself. If you try to make the right choices in your life and do your best to be kind to others, you will stand tall, no matter how short or tall you may be physically.

The Bible tells us a story about a short man who learned this lesson the hard way.

※   ※   ※

"How could any man have so much and yet be so unhappy?" Zacchaeus kept asking himself as he rested on his couch in his elegant home in Jericho. He was one of the richest Jews in the city. But he had hardly any friends, and he was very lonely.

As he thought back to his childhood, he realized that even then he had seldom been happy. He had been small for his age — undersized.

So he had been left out of games and had been generally unpopular — he hadn't been invited to parties. How often he had heard, "He's too little!"

"Shorty" had been his nickname. His real name, *Zacchaeus*, meant "righteous" or "just." That was a nice name. But "Shorty" was just awful!

So he had given up trying to make friends and had become more and more of a loner. Spending more time by himself, he had grown increasingly jealous and resentful of others. Although he had held in his anger, he had wished for some way to get even with those who made fun of him.

Now, as an adult, he had found a way. He was still a short person, less than five feet tall. But he was also a tax collector. In that position he took devilish delight in collecting taxes from his former schoolmates who had left him out of their games and called him "Shorty." Many times he had charged them more than they actually owed, which is how he had become richer and richer.

But in another way he had become poorer and poorer. The few friends he had made liked him less and less, while his enemies hated him more and more. Behind his back, and sometimes even to his face, they called him "Swindler." He hated that nickname even more than "Shorty," but he really deserved it because of the way he cheated people on their taxes. They also called him "Traitor" because he collected taxes for the Romans, who made life hard for the Jews. No wonder he felt so lonely and unhappy as he rested on his soft couch!

Zacchaeus's troubled thoughts were suddenly interrupted by loud shouting not far away. He sent a servant to find out the cause. A few minutes later the servant came back and reported that a famous teacher by the name of Jesus, with a band of twelve disciples, was approaching.

"He's on his way to Jerusalem to celebrate the Passover feast," said the servant. "A large crowd has gathered on both sides of the street to see him pass by."

"I've heard of him," said Zacchaeus. "I must see him, too!" He jumped up from his couch and hurried out. But when he reached the main street, he couldn't see over the heads of the crowd. And no one made way for him or even spoke to him. So he ran on ahead to a sycamore tree beside the street. Grasping one of the branches, he climbed to a point several feet above the crowd. Now he had what might be called a ringside seat, where he could see everything but wouldn't be noticed by anyone.

As Jesus came near, Zacchaeus noticed the strength of his stride, his noble face, and the warmth of his smile. No wonder the people were so enthusiastic! Those twelve strong men walking close to him were so fortunate to be his disciples! Zacchaeus almost wished he were one of them.

Then came the moment when Jesus was passing right under the tree. But no! Not passing — he was stopping! Looking up into the tree, Jesus called him by name! "Zacchaeus!" he said. "Come down! Hurry! I'm going home with you today!"

Zacchaeus couldn't believe his ears! Never before had anyone spoken to him like that. None of his neighbors or business acquaintances had ever said they wanted to visit him at home. For years he had been ignored, laughed at, rejected, and hated by the Jews for being a tax collector for the Romans.

And now, all of a sudden, here was this famous, popular teacher saying, in effect, "Of all the people in Jericho, you're the one I would like to know."

Of course Zacchaeus hurried down from the tree. Of course he welcomed Jesus warmly. He did it "joyfully," the Bible says. As he and Jesus walked toward his home, he was happier than he had ever been. He heard some of the people muttering about Jesus going home with the big swindler, a man who was a sinner, but he was too happy to care.

The Bible doesn't tell us what Jesus and Zacchaeus talked about that night. Possibly Zacchaeus found the courage to tell Jesus how unhappy he had been all his life because he was so small. Perhaps he told Jesus how unhappy he still was in spite of his wealth.

And perhaps Jesus quietly told Zacchaeus how much good he could do for poor people with his wealth, and that his real problem was not his size, but his attitude — that he had allowed himself to become resentful and unforgiving, selfish and greedy, and that it was what was inside that was making him miserable, not what was outside.

While we don't know what Jesus said to Zacchaeus during their conversation, we do know that as a result of it Zacchaeus became a different man. Before Jesus and Zacchaeus went to bed that night, Zacchaeus said to Jesus, "I'm going to change my selfish ways right away. I'm going to give half of my wealth to the poor, and if I've overcharged anyone on his taxes, I'll give him back four times as much."

Then and there, Zacchaeus turned his life around and became a new and noble person. Jesus said that salvation had come to Zacchaeus's house, and he added, "I have come into the world to seek and to save the lost." One of the lost Jesus was referring to, of course, was Zacchaeus. Once lost and unhappy because of his anger, selfishness, and greed, he had put all of these feelings out of his heart and allowed Jesus to come in instead. Zacchaeus was still physically short, but now he was standing tall.

Prayer

Dear God, keep me from being hurt by or angry toward anyone who may mistreat me or make fun of me. And help me always to treat others, especially those who may be mistreated or neglected, as I myself like to be treated. Make me thoughtful and kind as Jesus was. Help me to stand tall. In Jesus' name, amen.

Questions

1. Why was Zacchaeus so unhappy?
2. What does the name *Zacchaeus* mean?
3. How did Zacchaeus "get even" with those who had been mean to him when he was a boy?
4. Why couldn't Zacchaeus see Jesus as he passed through Jericho? What did he do about it?
5. Why do you think Jesus wanted to go home with Zacchaeus?
6. What do you suppose they talked about that night?
7. How do you know Zacchaeus became a changed man?
8. In what ways do you think you need to be changed?
9. How can Jesus do for you what he did for Zacchaeus?

Peer Pressure

John 3:1-21; 7:47-52; 19:38-47

What is "peer pressure"? It's the pressure that your friends, also called your peers, sometimes put on you to do something that you know you shouldn't do.

Sometimes your friends might encourage you to smoke a cigarette or take a drink or experiment with drugs — when you know that doing any of these things would hurt your health and your reputation. If you're afraid of being called "chicken," if you follow the crowd instead of your conscience, if you put what's popular ahead of what's right, if "standing *in*" with your friends is more important than "standing *up*" for what you believe — if any or all of these things is true of you, then you have a problem with peer pressure.

This story is about a man who had such a problem and how he struggled with it.

❧　　　❧　　　❧

Nicodemus had heard a great deal about Jesus and was curious about him, so he made up his mind to go to see him when he heard that Jesus was in Jerusalem for the Passover. Nicodemus was a Pharisee, and his closest friends were Pharisees too. The Pharisees were a religious group who, in Jesus' time, had a great deal of influence with the Jewish people. They were very strict in their interpretation of the Ten Commandments and other Old Testament laws, and they openly criticized Jesus for doing such things as healing on the Sabbath. Some had even threatened to kill Jesus if he came to Jerusalem for the Passover feast. Nicodemus knew that he himself would be criticized for going to see Jesus. That explains why he decided to go by night. He wanted to keep his visit a secret.

Once he had arrived at the house where Jesus was staying and had been welcomed by Jesus, Nicodemus said, "Teacher, we've heard here in Jerusalem about your mighty miracles in Galilee, and we know God must be with you. I've come to learn more about what you believe and teach."

Jesus gave an answer that wasn't at all what Nicodemus expected. "Nicodemus," he said, "let me tell you something as plainly as I can: Unless you are born again, you cannot enter the kingdom of heaven."

Nicodemus was startled, even shocked. After all, the Pharisees were the religious leaders of their day, and they were very proud and quite satisfied with themselves.

Jesus was reminding Nicodemus that, regardless of his good opinion about himself and regardless of his good reputation in Jerusalem, he needed to become a new and entirely different person if he was truly going to be saved. Nicodemus didn't understand. "What do you mean?" he asked Jesus.

"You are a teacher of Israel," answered Jesus, "and still you don't understand?" Jesus offered another explanation. "Nicodemus," he said, "do you remember that story in the book of Exodus about some of the people of Israel being bitten by snakes out in the wilderness? God told Moses to make a bronze snake and attach it to a pole, and those who looked up to the bronze snake in faith were saved. Well, one of these days," he continued, "I will be lifted up in the same way, so that everyone who believes in me may be saved."

Then, speaking very earnestly and looking straight into Nicodemus's eyes, Jesus added, "For God loved the world so much that he gave his only Son so that everyone who believes in him may have eternal life. Nicodemus, God sent me into the world not to be the world's judge, but to be the world's savior!"

At that very moment Jesus was opening the door of the kingdom of heaven to Nicodemus, offering to be his Savior and inviting him to become one of his followers. Why didn't Nicodemus do it? Was it because of "peer pressure"? Because he knew what his friends, the Pharisees, would say? How sad that he passed up this great opportunity to say "yes" to Jesus' earnest invitation! So the night was dark — very dark, and in more ways than one — as Nicodemus made his way back home.

In the days that followed, Nicodemus kept thinking about his visit with Jesus but couldn't find the courage to say anything to his friends about it. However, one day some weeks later, several of the Pharisees were discussing Jesus in front of Nicodemus when one of them said with a sneer, "Is there a single one of us who believes that he is the Messiah? The stupid crowds from Galilee may think he is, but what do they know? We Pharisees know better!"

That was too much for Nicodemus. Remembering how kind Jesus had been to him, and recalling Jesus' claim that he was the world's

Savior, Nicodemus broke in: "Is it fair to condemn a man before he has had a chance to speak for himself?"

Then one of the Pharisees let him have it: "Are you one of the stupid Galileans, too?" he sneered. "Read what is written in the Scriptures! No prophet ever came from Galilee!"

When he heard that, Nicodemus drew back into his shell. The "peer pressure" was on, and he didn't have the courage to resist it.

There was one other Pharisee in Jerusalem who, like Nicodemus, admired Jesus very much, and who also kept quiet about it for the same reason Nicodemus did. His name was Joseph, and in the Gospel of John he is described as "a secret disciple of Jesus because of his fear of the Jewish leaders."

We don't know just when he and

Nicodemus met, or when they shared with each other their personal interest in Jesus. But we do know that on the day Jesus was crucified, these two men decided they would be "secret" disciples no longer! It's possible that they were standing side by side near the cross as Jesus breathed his last when they made that decision and agreed what each would do.

So away they hurried — Joseph to get permission from Pilate to take Jesus' body down from the cross and bury it, and Nicodemus to purchase white linen sheets in which to wrap the body and fragrant ointment and spices to embalm it.

When the two men returned to Calvary and were standing at the foot of the cross, Nicodemus said, "Joseph, now I understand what he meant when he said to me, 'I will be lifted up from the earth so that everyone who believes in me may be saved.'"

Then they loosened the nails, tenderly lifted the body of Jesus from the cross, and lowered it to the ground. There they wrapped it in layer after layer of linen, made fragrant with the abundance of ointment and spices that Nicodemus had brought. All the while they were hearing shouts of ridicule and scorn from the crowd still milling around the hill. But they didn't mind. What they were doing amounted to a public vote against the decision of the Jewish rulers to condemn Jesus. They were doing what even his disciples, now in hiding, hadn't dared to do. No longer did they care what the Jewish leaders might say. "Peer pressure" didn't matter anymore! The one thing that did matter was Jesus and their devotion to him. They wanted all the world to know that they believed in him, loved him, and intended to be his faithful disciples as long as they lived — were ready to die for him, if need be!

But, as they later walked home in the gathering darkness, having laid Jesus' body to rest in the tomb Joseph had provided, they weren't thinking of their final courageous deed. They were thinking instead about what cowards they had been earlier! They had done what they could, but there was so much more they might have done for him and for his cause if they hadn't waited until that last dark hour to declare their faith. It was so little and so late, when he had given so much!

Prayer

Dear God, it's so easy to give in to peer pressure. When I feel its power, help me to resist it and to do what's right. Give me the strength and the courage I need to stand always against the wrong. In Jesus' name, amen.

Questions

1. Explain what "peer pressure" is and give examples from your own experience.
2. Who were the Pharisees, and what were they like?
3. Why did Nicodemus want to visit Jesus? Why did he go at night?
4. What did Jesus tell Nicodemus he needed, and what did Jesus mean?
5. What did Jesus invite Nicodemus to do, and why didn't he accept the invitation?
6. In what way were Nicodemus and his friend Joseph alike?
7. Tell about the burial of Jesus and what each of the two men did.

8. What was their one regret as they walked home together?
9. "Procrastination," someone said, is "putting off until tomorrow what you should have done yesterday." Discuss how this applies to Nicodemus and Joseph and how you can keep it from applying to you.

Almost Too Good to Be True

John 4

The brightest and happiest day of your life! — what would you say it was? A birthday when you received a wonderful surprise? A Christmas when you were showered with more gifts than you knew what to do with? Or perhaps the day when something happened that changed your life for the better? Whatever your answer, you will be interested in this story about a woman whose brightest and happiest day was the day she met Jesus. But it didn't start off as a bright day . . .

❧   ❧   ❧

We don't know her name, so let's call her Mara. The name means "bitter," and that was the way she felt almost every day of her life — bitter toward the women of her village for the way they avoided her, bitter toward the men of her village for the way they treated her and talked about her, bitter toward herself for the mess she had made of her life.

On this particular day, she didn't want to see anyone. That's why she waited until noon to go down to the well with her pitcher to get the supply of water she needed for the rest of the day. There was only one well in Sychar, the village where she lived, and all the other women went to the well early in the morning while it was still cool. To Mara,

the one advantage of going in the heat of the day was that no one else would be there! Or so she thought. But she was wrong.

When she arrived, she discovered a man sitting beside the well. She hesitated a moment, wishing he wasn't there. But she was relieved to note that he was a stranger. At least he wouldn't know her past and wouldn't treat her with scorn like most of the men in her village did.

As she set her pitcher down and prepared to lower the bucket into the well, the stranger spoke to her politely and asked if she would give him a drink.

Immediately she recognized that he was a Jew. She herself was a Samaritan, and the Jews didn't get along with the Samaritans. They had serious religious differences that kept them apart. Usually the Jews didn't even speak to the Samaritans.

So Mara was amazed that this Jewish stranger should ask her for a drink of water. "How is it that you, a Jew, ask me, a Samaritan woman, for a drink?" she replied.

But she was even more amazed at Jesus' answer: "If you only knew the gift that God has for you, and who I am, you would ask me for a drink of living water."

"But sir," she said, "this is a deep well, and you don't have either a rope or a bucket. Where would you get that living water?"

Then Jesus went on to explain that the water he was able to give was far better than the water that comes from the earth. "It is the water of eternal life," he said, "and it becomes like an ever-flowing spring within a person. Everyone who drinks of it never becomes thirsty again!"

This made Mara eager to taste it. "Please, sir, give me some of that water! Then I won't have to make this long walk to the well every day."

"Go get your husband and return here," Jesus instructed.

"But I don't have a husband," said Mara, and her voice was troubled.

"That's true in a way," Jesus answered, "but you have had five husbands, and you aren't married to the man you live with now."

Mara was silent for a moment. She was so ashamed she didn't know what to say. How did this stranger know about the mess she had made of her life? She decided to change the subject.

"You seem to be a prophet," she said, "so tell me why you Jews teach that the temple in Jerusalem is the only place to worship God. We Samaritans believe that the mountain where our temple stood before it was destroyed over a hundred years ago is also a holy place."

"It isn't *where* we worship but *how* we worship that counts with God," Jesus answered. "It isn't the *place* that matters, but the *spirit* in which we worship."

Mara replied, "I know when the Messiah comes — and I believe with all my heart that he *is* coming — he will explain everything that we don't understand."

"He has already come," Jesus answered. "I am the Messiah."

Mara's face lit up with joyful amazement. Now she understood why this man had treated her with such kindness and also why he knew everything about her past.

Just then Jesus' disciples arrived. They had been in the village to buy food. But Mara hardly noticed them. Not bothering to pick up her water jar, she hurried back to the village to tell the people about this man and what he had said to her.

When the people of the village heard the news, they followed Mara back to the well. As they visited with Jesus, they were so impressed that they forgot all about the prejudice between Jews and Samaritans, and they invited him and his disciples to stay in their village as their guests. Jesus and his disciples accepted — and stayed for two whole days!

After that, the other villagers said to Mara, "At first we believed because of what you said about him. But now that we've listened to him, we know for sure that he *is* the Messiah, the Savior of the world."

Mara knew it too, and though her name didn't change, she did. No longer could it be said that her life was "bitter" because, of all the people in Sychar, she was the happiest! Not only had she met her Savior, but she now understood what he meant when he spoke about giving her the water of eternal life to drink. It seemed almost too good to be true — but it wasn't!

Prayer

Dear God, you know what a sinner I am, and yet you love me just the same. Please forgive me when I go astray, and keep me on the straight and upward path to your kingdom. Help me to be always thirsty for the living water you offer me. In Jesus' name, amen.

Questions

1. Why did Mara wait until noon to go to the well for water?
2. Who was there when she arrived, and what did he ask her to do?
3. What did Jesus offer to give Mara, and what did he mean?
4. Why was Mara ashamed of her past life?

5. What did Jesus tell Mara about where people should worship God?
6. What did Jesus tell Mara that amazed her, and what did she do?
7. How did Mara feel after she met Jesus?
8. Discuss what it means for us to receive the "water of eternal life" from Jesus.

The Best Gift of All

John 9

The saying "We never know how good water is until the well goes dry" reminds us of how easy it is to take our blessings for granted and not to appreciate them until we perhaps lose them. Try this experiment, for example:

Close your eyes very tightly and slowly count to sixty — in other words, keep your eyes closed for about a minute. Now, before you open them, imagine that you couldn't see — that you had to spend the rest of your life behind that veil of darkness.

Then ask God to make you truly grateful for your eyes, which allow you to do so much — to look at all the beautiful things in the world, to see other people, to be able to read books, to walk or run without fear of falling.

This story is about a man — we'll call him Peter — who never knew how wonderful the gift of sight was until . . .

❧   ❧   ❧

Peter was amazed at everything he saw! The sky was a brilliant blue, the sun a shining gold. The grass and trees were a vivid green, and the flowers were the colors of the rainbow — red, blue, and yellow. Now he knew what the people he had known all his life — his parents, his friends, his neighbors — looked like! Yes, of course he was amazed! For up to this time he had been blind, but now he could see!

It had all come about because of a man named Jesus. Although Peter had never met him, he had heard a great deal about him. Then one day Jesus came by the street corner in Jerusalem where Peter sat, tin cup in hand, begging for coins from passersby. But Jesus didn't pass him by. He stopped and spoke kindly to Peter about his blindness. Then, saying to his disciples, "As long as I am in the world, I am the light of the world," he put a mud pack on Peter's eyes. "Now, go to the pool of Siloam and wash off the mud," Jesus instructed him, "and you will be healed."

Deep in his heart Peter felt this newfound friend meant what he said. Half-believing and half-hoping, Peter made his way to the pool of Siloam, which wasn't far away. Sure enough, as he washed the mud away and opened his eyes, he found he could see!

"Hallelujah! God be praised!" he shouted as he threw his tin cup away. Soon he began to go from house to house, joyfully telling his neighbors what had happened.

"Do you remember me?" he asked. "Once I was blind, but now I can see!" And he told them how he had been healed.

Some of the people he talked to did remember him as the blind beggar who sat on the street corner with his tin cup. They congratulated him on his newfound joy.

But others said, "You do look like the beggar from the corner, but you couldn't be that man. He was really blind!"

"But I am that man!" Peter insisted, and he told them again how his sight had been restored.

Later, some who still doubted his story took him to the synagogue to see the Pharisees, a religious group of very strict people who were against Jesus and always eager to find something to criticize him about. Peter told the Pharisees the same story about Jesus healing him.

"On what day did he do this?" they asked him.

"On the Sabbath," Peter replied, "the day I went to the temple to worship."

"Aha!" snorted one of the Pharisees. "So he broke the fourth commandment — he did something that involved labor on the Sabbath. That makes him a sinner, not a man sent from God. So your story doesn't hold water. Now tell us the truth about what happened."

"I've told you the truth over and over," Peter insisted. "How many more times do I have to repeat it before you believe it?"

"But we've just proved that the man is a sinner," another Pharisee insisted.

"That's your opinion!" Peter said with anger in his voice. "The one thing I'm sure about is that once I was blind, but now I can see!"

"Who do you think this Jesus is?" they challenged him.

"He must be a prophet of God," Peter answered, "because it was by God's power that he opened my eyes."

After that the Pharisees even asked Peter's parents about his healing. In the end they were convinced that Peter had been blind, but they refused to believe that Jesus had healed him. So they sent for Peter a second time and challenged him again.

"Give God the praise for your healing," they insisted. "We know this man Jesus is a sinner."

But Peter refused. "If this man were not from God," he argued, "he wouldn't have been able to heal me."

By this time the Pharisees realized that they couldn't make Peter change his story. So they did a very cruel thing. Speaking for all of them, their leader said, "Since you're so determined to stand up for this fellow Jesus, you will no longer be welcome in the synagogue." Then they put him out of the synagogue and took his name off the list of members.

But that isn't the end of the story. Because Jesus did something that was as kind as the Pharisees' deed was cruel. Having heard how Peter had been treated by the Pharisees, Jesus inquired about where he was and went to see him. Up to this time, remember, Peter really didn't know who Jesus was. He had never seen him, either, because he had been blind the first time they met.

So imagine what a thrill it was for Peter now to look into Jesus' face and to realize that Jesus cared about him enough to go to the trouble of seeking him out. How warmly Peter must have greeted and thanked Jesus once he knew who he was!

We don't know what Jesus and Peter actually said to each other at the beginning of their conversation, but before long, Peter found out that he was about to receive from Jesus a blessing even greater than the recovery of his sight. For Jesus said to him, "Do you believe in the Son of God?"

"Who is he, Lord?" the man answered. "For with all my heart I want to believe in him!"

"You are looking into his face now," Jesus replied, "and you are talking to him."

Falling upon his knees and looking gratefully into Jesus' eyes, Peter said, "Lord, I do believe in you. You are the Light of the world and my Savior!"

From that time on, it didn't matter to Peter what the Pharisees thought or said, or that he had been banned from the synagogue. Because now he knew that Jesus was the Son of God and his personal Savior and Friend. And that was the best gift of all!

Prayer

Dear God, help me to appreciate the many gifts I often take for granted — the gifts of sight and speech, of taste and touch and smell. But help me to appreciate most the gift of Christ that you sent to the world. In Jesus' name, amen.

Questions

1. How did Jesus heal Peter's blindness?
2. What did Peter do after he was healed?
3. Why did some of the people who saw Peter after he was healed take him to the Pharisees?
4. How did the Pharisees respond to Peter's claim that he had been healed?
5. What did Jesus do later?
6. How do you think you would respond to seeing a miracle today?
7. How can we keep from taking God's gifts to us — like sight — for granted?
8. How can we keep from taking the gift of Christ for granted?

A Diamond in the Rough

Matthew 16:13-24; Luke 22:31-34, 54-62

The diamond, as you know, is a very beautiful and a very valuable precious stone. Most likely it is the jewel in the ring your father gave to your mother when they became engaged to be married.

But quite a few things were done with that diamond before it was mounted in your mother's ring. Its "life" began, we might say, as "a diamond in the rough." First, someone had to find it — and someone did, perhaps in a dark mine way down below the surface of the earth in South Africa. After it was found, it had to be separated from the sand and dirt, possibly from a hard lump of ore in which it had become embedded, and finally put into the hands of a lapidary.

A lapidary is a skillful jeweler who can do amazing things with precious stones. When he is about to work on an uncut diamond, he studies it carefully with two aims in mind. First, he wants to cut out of the rough stone the largest and most perfect stone possible. Second, he wants to remove any and every flaw or defect in the stone.

In the story that follows, you'll see that Jesus was a kind of lapidary.

[209]

When Jesus was on earth, he put a great deal of effort into his relationship with his disciples. You might say he worked with them the way a lapidary works with diamonds. Most certainly they were "diamonds in the rough" at the beginning. During the three years they were together, sometimes they were an inspiration to Jesus, and sometimes they were a problem. But all the while they were not only learning but being changed for the better.

Take the disciple whose name was Simon Peter, for example.

One day near the end of his ministry Jesus was sitting with his disciples in a quiet place. He said to them, "Who do the people think I am?"

"Some think one thing and some another," the disciples replied. "Some say you're John the Baptist, whom King Herod beheaded, risen from the dead. Some say you're one of the prophets or Elijah sent by God to prepare the way for the coming of the Christ."

Jesus was leading up to the all-important question. After a pause he said, "But what about you? Who do you say I am?"

It was Simon Peter who broke in with a strong answer: "Master, you are the Christ, the Son of the living God."

Jesus was deeply moved, not only by what Peter had said but by the forceful way in which he had said it.

"It was my Father in heaven who revealed this truth to you!" Jesus said in reply, "and bless you for saying it!" Then he added, "Your name has been 'Simon,' but from now on it will be 'Peter,' which means 'Rock.' You will be the foundation on which I will build my church, and not even the gates of hell will be able to stand against it!"

On that day Peter was an inspiration to Jesus! But that would soon change.

A few days later Jesus was trying to explain to his disciples that since he was the Christ, as Peter had said, he would have to go to Jerusalem and suffer and die in order to become the world's Savior. His words came as a shock to all of them! Up to this time they had expected him to become their king on earth and wear a crown, not die on a cross!

Again it was Peter who spoke up, but this time his words were just the opposite of what Jesus needed to hear.

"Oh, no!" he exclaimed. "Surely you don't mean what you're saying! Dying on a cross? That could never happen to you!"

Jesus answered Peter very sternly. This time he called him a name very different from "Peter, the Rock."

"Get away from me, Satan! You are a stumbling block to me when what I need is a stepping-stone! It is not what you would have me do that I must keep in mind, but what my Father in heaven would have me do!"

In this situation, Peter was a problem to Jesus, not an inspiration. And this wasn't the last time he was a problem.

It was the last night before Jesus' crucifixion. Jesus had spent the evening with his disciples in a friend's home, where he had performed the service of communion for the first time. After that, Jesus and his disciples went to the Garden of Gethsemane, where Jesus was going to pray. At the gate of the garden, Jesus stopped. Turning to his disciples, he said with great sadness in his voice, "Tomorrow all of you will desert me, like sheep running in all directions when their shepherd is killed!"

Again Peter broke in: "I won't!" he exclaimed. "No matter what these others may do, I will never desert you! You can count on me, no matter what happens."

But Jesus, knowing by now what a wishy-washy person Peter was,

replied, "Listen, Peter, as I tell you the truth! This very night, before the rooster crows in the morning to announce the dawn, you will deny me three times."

"No, never!" Peter exclaimed. "Even if I have to die with you, I will never deny you!"

And of course he meant it. It was the hero in his soul that was talking. But there was a coward in his soul too. Like all of us, Peter was a "two-in-one" person, and later that night the coward took command.

Shortly after that, Jesus was arrested. He was taken to the house of the high priest, where he was put on trial before the Jewish leaders. Peter had followed behind at a safe distance and was sitting near a fire in the yard with the soldiers who had arrested Jesus, trying to keep warm and hoping he wouldn't be recognized.

But a young woman noticed him and, looking him over, said, "This man was with Jesus."

That moment was Peter's big opportunity to stand up for Jesus, to say, "Yes, I was, and that's why I'm here. I know he's innocent and should be set free. He should never have been arrested!" But instead Peter said, "You're crazy. I don't even know him." A little later, a man came by and said, as he looked at Peter, "I know this man was with Jesus!" But again Peter denied that he even knew Jesus.

About an hour later, someone standing around the fire looked him straight in the face and said, "You must be one of his followers. From the way you talk, anybody can tell you're from Galilee, and that's where Jesus is from."

By now Peter was really in a tight corner. He was so nervous that he swore, then added, "I'm telling you, I don't even know the man. I've never even seen him before!"

Just at that instant, a rooster crowed nearby. And in a flash it all came back to Peter — the words of warning Jesus had spoken to him just a few hours before. Too ashamed to speak, Peter got up and started to leave. On the way out, he looked up toward the room where Jesus was being questioned by the Jewish leaders, and Jesus was looking straight at him. That look melted Peter's heart. He left the courtyard, leaned against a tree outside, and cried.

And we may be sure he also prayed, asking over and over to be forgiven for being such a coward and wondering if he would ever become the man Jesus had in mind when he said, "Your name will be Peter, which means 'Rock'!"

The happy ending to this story is that in time Peter did become just that — a rock, a strong person who helped build the foundation of the church. In the book of Acts he is the leader of the disciples who goes from place to place preaching, teaching, and healing as Jesus had done. More than once we read of how courageous he was.

Perhaps the struggle in Peter's soul between the coward and the hero was with him until the end of his life. But even if it was, because of the kind of Savior Jesus was to him, we may be sure that it was the hero that finally won out. A "diamond in the rough" was transformed by a skillful and patient lapidary into a sparkling jewel!

Prayer

Dear God, I know I'm a lot like Peter — that I have both a hero and a coward inside me. Help me to be a hero, to be strong and true to you. But those times when I'm a coward, please be patient with me. Help me to become a brighter and brighter diamond for you. In Jesus' name, amen.

Questions

1. When Jesus asked his disciples "Who do you think I am?" what did Peter say?
2. Explain the meaning of Peter's name and why Jesus gave it to him.
3. What did Peter say when Jesus spoke about dying, and what did Jesus say in reply?
4. What did Peter say when Jesus predicted that his disciples were going to desert him?
5. What was Jesus' answer?
6. Describe what happened to Peter when he was sitting by the fire trying to keep warm.
7. Why did he leave? Where did he go? What did he do?
8. In what ways are you a diamond in the rough?
9. Can Jesus help you polish off your rough edges? If so, how, and how can you participate in this process?

From "Hothead" to "Apostle of Love"

Mark 9:38-41; Luke 9:51-56; John 19:25-27

Do you ever watch tennis matches on television? If you do, you've probably heard Bjorn Borg's name mentioned. At his best, he was one of the top players in the world.

Once I watched him in a championship tournament. Sitting not more than thirty or forty feet away, I was amazed at his terrific serves, his smooth strokes — both forehand and backhand — and his calmness under pressure. They called him "the Iceman," and I could see why. He never got upset when he missed a shot, never questioned the call of a linesman or the umpire.

But he wasn't always like that. When he was a little boy learning to play the game, he had an ugly temper. Sometimes when he missed a shot, he would slam the ball against the fence or throw his racquet down.

Then his mother, who very much wanted him to become a good

player, would take his racquet away from him, sometimes for a week at a time, and give him a lecture. "Bjorn," she would say, "if you don't learn to control yourself, you'll never be able to control your racquet!" In time he learned that lesson and became a true champion.

This story is about a man who, like Bjorn Borg, had a hard time learning how to control his temper, but who was fortunate to have a very wonderful teacher.

Had we known what he was like when Jesus called him to be one of his twelve disciples, we might have wondered why Jesus ever chose him. Or, having chosen him, why Jesus didn't send him back home and choose someone else. His name was John, and at the beginning of his relationship with Jesus, he apparently had a bad temper.

His brother James did too. So, as a way to scold them and remind them of the worst flaw in their character, Jesus gave them a very appropriate Hebrew nickname, "Boanerges." In English that means "Sons of Thunder" or "Hotheads." No doubt Jesus used that nickname quite often when one or both of the brothers lost their temper!

But there were other times when Jesus had to be more direct and firm. For example, there was the time when John saw a man trying to drive an evil spirit out of an afflicted man by using the name of Jesus. Rushing up to the man, John shouted, "Who are you to use the name of Jesus in trying to work a miracle? You have no right to use his name when you're not one of his disciples!"

"You take care of your business, and I'll take care of mine!" the man shouted back, and he kept on trying to heal the sick man.

John was still boiling mad when he reported to Jesus what had happened. "Master," he said, "I did my best to get him to stop because he wasn't one of your followers, but he wouldn't listen!"

John waited, expecting Jesus to support him for what he had tried to do. But instead, he heard Jesus say, "My dear friend, when will you ever learn not to criticize other people? Remember what I said in my sermon on the mountain in Galilee: 'Do not judge others, for in the same way you judge, you will be judged. . . . In everything treat others as you would have others treat you.' Don't you see that if the man was trying to heal in my name, it means he's on our side, whether he knows it or not? You should have tried to help him, not stop him."

There was another day when both John and his brother James needed and received a still more severe scolding. Jesus and his disciples were on their way to Jerusalem to observe the Passover. They needed a place to stay for the night, so Jesus sent John and James on ahead to make arrangements in the next village, which was a Samaritan village. But the two disciples were turned down everywhere they went, because the Samaritans were religiously prejudiced against the Jews.

When John and James returned and reported to Jesus how they had been turned away again and again, John said, with flashing eyes, "Master, shall we call down fire from heaven and burn them up?"

Perhaps it was at this point that Jesus first nicknamed the two brothers "Boanerges." They called for lightning from heaven, so Jesus called them "Thunderclaps." In any case, Jesus spoke to them very sternly: "What a horrible suggestion! Shame on you to even think of it!" He paused, then asked in a pleading voice, "When will you learn that God sent me into the world not to kill people but to save them?" Then Jesus led the disciples to another village where they found a place to stay for the night.

We don't know just how often Jesus had to scold John about his temper, but we do know that they were together as teacher and disciple for three years. And eventually John learned not only to control his anger but to replace it with love and gentleness. For proof of that, we go in our imaginations to Calvary.

There, as we read in the Gospel which John himself later wrote, Jesus, as he was dying, looked down and saw his mother and John standing side by side at the foot of the cross. According to the Gospels, John was the only one of the twelve disciples who had the courage to stand by Jesus when he was being tried and also the only one who was with him when he was dying.

So now Jesus, looking down from the cross, saw John and his mother standing together. With a heart full of love for his mother and full of trust in John, he said, "John,

my dear friend, take her and care for her as if she were your own mother."

And to Mary, Jesus said, "Mother, go and live with John as if he were your own son."

Then and there John put his arms around Mary, and a short while later, with her leaning on his arm, he took her to his home. There, we may be sure, he cared for her as lovingly and tenderly as if she had been his own mother.

It is not surprising, is it, that from then on John was known as "the Apostle of Love." In a letter he later wrote, which appears in the Bible, he said, "Dear friends, let us practice loving each other, for love comes from God, and those who are loving and kind show that they are the children of God. . . . God is love, and everyone who lives in love is living in God, and God is living in him. For though we have never seen God, when we love each other, God lives in us and his love within us grows ever stronger" (1 John 4:7, 16, 12, Living Bible).

How did a man who was a hothead when he first met Jesus in time become "the Apostle of Love"? The explanation can be given in one sentence: In Jesus, John had a warm friend and a wonderful teacher, and in John, Jesus had a student who listened and obeyed.

Wouldn't we all be wise to enroll in "the School of Jesus," as John did, and to keep on learning and improving as long as we live?

Prayer

Dear God, please forgive me when I lose my temper and say something I shouldn't. Help me to keep my temper and my tongue under control, and to become more loving each day. In Jesus' name, amen.

Questions

1. What was John's chief problem when he became a disciple of Jesus?
2. What nickname did Jesus give John and his brother James, and what did the name mean? Why was it appropriate?
3. What did Jesus say when John told him about trying to stop the man who was trying to heal a sick man?
4. What did John want to do to the Samaritans who were unwilling to give Jesus and his disciples a room for the night?
5. What was Jesus' reply?
6. When Jesus was being tried and crucified, what did John do that none of the other disciples did?
7. When Jesus spoke to John from the cross, what did he ask him to do?
8. What was John called from that time on?
9. Jesus helped John learn to control his temper. How can Jesus do the same thing for us that he did for John? How can we participate in this process?

Working Together for Good

Mark 15:21-24; Romans 16:13

In the Bible there is one promise that sounds almost too good to be true. It is in Romans 8:28, which says, "God makes all things work together for good for those who love him."

Can that always be true? What about the sincere Christian whose home is swept away by a flood or destroyed by fire? Or who loses a leg or an arm in a car accident? Or who loses a job and can't find another one?

But notice the promise doesn't say that "*everything* works for the good of those who love God"; it says that "all things *working together* are for their good."

Someday you may be sick. After examining you, the doctor will write out a prescription, and your mother will take it to the druggist to get it filled. As the druggist reads the prescription, he may realize that one of the substances by itself would be harmful to you, but combined with the other substances called for by the doctor, it will make a medicine that will help you to become strong and well again.

When all the substances work together, the result will be for your good!

This story is about a man who one day was forced to do something that he didn't want to do. In fact, he was very angry with those people who made him do it. At the time, he couldn't understand why God would allow this to happen to him, because he was a very religious man.

But years later, looking back, he thanked God that it did happen and for the many other ways God had made things work together for his good and for the good of his family.

❧   ❧   ❧

For Simon the day had begun bright with promise. The sun was shining, the birds were singing, and he was at peace with himself and with the world.

He had spent the night in an inn outside Jerusalem, since the city was overcrowded with visitors who had come from far and near to celebrate the Jewish Passover. Simon himself had traveled from far away — all the way from the city of Cyrene in North Africa, which was over a thousand miles from Jerusalem. On the evening before, he had shared the Passover meal with a number of other Jews in the inn where he had found lodging. Already he was feeling homesick for his wife and his two sons, Alexander and Rufus, back in Cyrene. But before setting out for home, religious man that he was, he decided to return to the temple in Jerusalem for one more time of worship before leaving the city.

It wasn't quite nine o'clock in the morning as he made his way toward the temple. He wanted to be there early so as not to miss any of the inspiring services associated with the Passover celebration. In joyful expectation his heart was singing, "I was glad when they said unto me, 'Let us go into the house of the Lord.'"

Just outside the city gate he found the street blocked by a huge procession of people moving in the opposite direction. At the front of the procession were three condemned men, each carrying a heavy wooden cross and being prodded along by a band of Roman soldiers.

One of the three men was noticeably different from the other two. It was plain that he had been horribly abused and was suffering greatly. But, in spite of this, there was a nobility in his face and a tender patience in his eyes such as Simon had never seen before.

The man was wearing a crown of thorns that had been pressed down hard on his brow, causing little streams of blood to trickle down on his forehead and cheeks. His back was bare, and it was bloody too — obviously he had been whipped in addition to being forced to wear the crown of thorns.

The cross he was carrying was heavy, and as he staggered past Simon, he stumbled and fell to his knees. Instinctively Simon reached out his hand to support the cross and to lift the pitiful man to his feet.

It was at that moment that Simon felt a strong hand gripping his shoulder and heard a stern voice say, "Hey, you! You're strong and healthy — you carry it for him!" It was one of the soldiers speaking.

"Yeah, let him carry it!" the other soldiers shouted. "After that whipping Pilate gave Jesus, he's a wreck!"

"But I'm not part of this crowd," Simon protested. "I was just passing by! I'm on my way to the temple for the morning sacrifice!"

"Good excuse," the first soldier replied, "but not good enough. An order is an order! Pick up his cross, and let's get going!"

The order was from a Roman soldier, and in that day Rome ruled

the world. So Simon had no choice but to obey. But how he resented having to do what the soldier had ordered! To carry that cross would make him an object of ridicule to the people in the procession. To some it would appear that he himself was a criminal on the way to his own execution. Others would think that he was in favor of executing this man Jesus, and would assume he was helping the process along. Who was this Jesus, anyway? Simon hadn't even known his name until he heard the soldier call him "Jesus."

But Simon was soon to learn who Jesus was and why he was being crucified — and he would learn that from the lips of Jesus himself. For as he carried that cross out to the hill of Calvary, where the three men would be executed, he was walking side by side with Jesus.

The Gospel writers don't tell us what Simon and Jesus said to one another as the procession moved along, but we can be sure of one thing: it wasn't a *silent* walk.

Somewhere along the way, Jesus must have told Simon the good news that we hear in John 3:16: that God so loved the world that he had sent Jesus, his only Son, to be the world's Savior, so that everyone who believed in him might not perish but have eternal life. Maybe Jesus said something like that after they arrived at Calvary, as he thanked Simon for carrying his cross.

It is quite possible that Simon was so touched by the things Jesus told him and was so drawn to Jesus that he couldn't leave once the procession had arrived at the hill. Perhaps he forgot all about going to the temple, as he had planned, and decided to stay with Jesus instead.

Perhaps Simon was standing near the cross when the robber dying beside Jesus prayed, "Jesus, remember me when you come into your kingdom." If so, Simon must have also heard Jesus' answer: "Truly I say to you, today you will be with me in paradise."

It is possible that at that very moment Jesus looked down and said to Simon, "I go to prepare a place for you too, Simon, that where I am, there you may be also." And when Christ breathed his last, it is possible that Simon said, along with the Roman officer who had been watching Christ, "Truly this man was the Son of God!"

We don't know just when or how it happened. But we do know

that it did happen — that on that first Good Friday over 1900 years ago, something "very good" happened to Simon. He met and came to know Jesus as his Savior and Lord!

So, he went back to Cyrene knowing not only that he had carried the cross for Jesus, but that Jesus had died on that cross for him! That was the wonderful story he had for his wife and two sons when he arrived back home a few days later.

And he told the story with such enthusiasm and gratitude that his wife and his children also became earnest believers in Jesus.

Some years later, Simon and his family moved to Rome, a city where it was by no means easy to be a Christian. In the church that had been established there, Simon's two sons, now grown young men, were well known and highly regarded as members of the church. In addition, Simon's wife became such a warm friend to the Apostle Paul that in his letter addressed to the church in Rome, written some thirty or forty years after the crucifixion of Jesus, he referred to her as his second mother (Romans 16:13)!

When you put all the parts of this story together, what would you say it teaches about "All things working together for good for those who love God"? To put it another way, what do you think Simon would say if he were here and were asked the same question?

I think he might say, "It's important to trust God even when you don't understand what's happening. I remember a day when I had had what I thought was a good plan. But my plan was interrupted, changed in a way that I didn't like, in a way that I resented, that made the day look bad to me! But now, looking back, I realize that that day turned out to be the most wonderful day of my entire life. It was the day I did something for Jesus and he did something for me that neither of us will ever forget!"

Prayer

Dear God, it's easy to love and trust you and to thank you for all your blessings when I'm happy and everything's going my way. But on a day when things go wrong, help me to remember that whatever trials you send, things are bound to come out right in the end. In Jesus' name, amen.

Questions

1. As our story begins, what was Simon planning to do?
2. What kept him from following his plan?
3. Describe the procession of people that he met.
4. How did he react when the Roman soldier ordered him to carry Jesus' cross?
5. What do you suppose he and Jesus talked about on their way to Calvary?
6. How do we know that Simon became a Christian?
7. What story did he tell his wife and sons when he returned to Cyrene, and what was the result?
8. What do we know about them when they were in Rome years later? (See Mark 15:21.)
9. How is this story related to the promise that "God makes all things work together for good for those who love him"?